WHAT THEY ARE SAYING...

To my amazement, I got through my son's college career without incurring any debt. As a wage-earning tradesman facing the complexity and high cost of higher education, I know that I got through it without losing my shirt only because of Joan and her methodology.

—Christopher Nord, Self-Employed, Newton, NH

My daughter and I found Joan very late in the game (literally within a few months of submitting applications). All three of us worked tirelessly and were able to submit a significant number of scholarship applications that were, in turn, awarded to my daughter. Without Joan, we never would have known how to present Gabby in such a beautiful, positive, and compelling way. In fact, the Greater Concord Board of Realtors, in their awards speech, mentioned that it was the most amazing application package they had ever seen.

—Darcy Howard, Bow, NH

Joan was able to help my daughter with funding for her Bachelor's and Master's degrees, and my son with funding for private high school and his Bachelor's Degree. My children received over $100,000 in outside private scholarships and grants. Joan helped us set up a repeatable process with standardized documents—her method really worked for us.

—Diane Valentine, Rye, NH

Ryan organized us! We were like any other young family, juggling ballet schedules, flute lessons, orchestra, school, double careers, and a dog! We knew we had raw talent in our kids—but it was Joan's portable accordion file system, assignments, and documentation that fleshed out the abstract applications. Joan's methods are challenging but once accomplished... the results are worth it!

—Grant Drumheller, Art Professor,
University of New Hampshire

Solely because of this service, my daughter founded her own Theatrical Society Chapter, attended the national conference in Nebraska, attended a fantastic experience at Girls' State and is prepared to qualify for every scholarship that matches our family background.

—Stephanie Burns, Lee, NH

On several occasions we received compliments regarding our packaged presentation of the applications. No matter how frustrating and aggravating financing college may get, Joan always said, "Keep a penny in your pocket. It says 'In God We Trust,'" We did that and still do trust the way Joan has led us through the college process.

—Joseph and Cathy Coco, Haverhill, MA

I would not have known how or where to begin the daunting task of locating scholarship money for my journey back to college as an adult student. My first step was to trust the process mapped out for me. Joan systematically, in a highly-organized fashion, led me "one piece of paper at a time" toward the end result—my own scholarship package.

—Judith McCann, Voice Teacher, Rye, NH

[Joan] is amazing. She has shown me opportunities in my own field (Developmentally Disabled) that I didn't even know existed and gave me the step–by-step directions to proceed. One of Joan's suggestions was a scholarship that was available in Sweden for a three-week course on the developmentally disabled... when you are done, you will feel empowered.

—Melissa Tremblay, Rye, NH

I invited Joan to speak to our single-parent group at the Technical College in Stratham, NH. Joan turned out to be someone who is knowledgeable, well organized, prepared, and articulate. She provided our students with a great deal of valuable information. I would not hesitate to refer anyone to Joan for assistance with seeking grants or scholarships.

—Sarah A. Scranton, Co-Coordinator,
Learning and Career Center,
New Hampshire Technical College at Stratham

As a guidance counselor with 25 years experience, I know that in every graduating high school class there are students who give up or limit their choice of colleges because of the lack of finances. Joan's program opens up opportunities to students to learn how to search and to take on the responsibility for their future education.

—Stephen C. Miller, Academic Advisor,
Portsmouth Center, New Hampshire College

SCHOLARSHIP MATTERS

A PARENT'S GUIDE TO COLLEGE AND PRIVATE SCHOLARSHIPS

JOAN CATHERINE RYAN

Mayflower Cottage Press
Hampton, NH

Mayflower Cottage Press
93 Winnacunnet Road, #3
Hampton, NH 03842

Cover and text design by Joyce C. Weston

ISBN 978-0-615-72066-1
Library of Congress Control Number: 2012954127

Printed in the United States of America

To my son, Eric W. Schwartz,
born February 17, 1971; passed away from
brain cancer April 20, 2012.

And to my granddaughter,
Zoe Catherine Meinen, born October 27, 2008;
diagnosed with brain cancer in August 2012.

Dedicated also to all children. Please repeat after me:

No matter what the circumstances of my life, no matter what I may have been told by others, or may have told myself about my worth or potential, today is the day to shake off my old self-image and know the truth. I am God's beloved child. God loves me and approves of me. I have the stamp of divine approval and success upon me.

God's love for me is so great that He has placed His Spirit within me, thus establishing unlimited potential within me. I have the stamp of divine approval and success upon me, for God's Spirit within ensures the fulfillment of my dreams and goals and desires. I have been created for greatness. Nothing can thwart or prevent the upward, progressive movement of my mind, my soul, and my life.

> *Thus says the Lord, who created you.*
> *"I have called you by name, you are mine.*
> *You are precious in my eyes,*
> *And honored, and I love you."*
> Isaiah 43:4

Reprinted with permission of Unity®, publisher of *The Daily Word*®

CONTENTS

CRITICAL STUDENT INFORMATION

STEP TWO: COLLEGE ADMISSION AND FINANCIAL AID

STEP THREE: EDUCATIONAL AND PRIVATE SCHOLARSHIP MONEY

APPENDIX

ACKNOWLEDGMENTS

To parents and students—the unsung, courageous, frontline, everyday warriors.

To the teachers, counselors, coaches, mentors, and grandparents we remember for the rest of our lives.

To small business owners whose selfless contributions toward private scholarships make it possible for students to remain in college year after year.

To the American Legion for its stalwart commitment to education for our youth.

To Northern Essex Community College (NECCO), Haverhill, Massachusetts, for always stepping up to the new economic reality and providing real-life, job-producing educational programs.

To friends like Martha and Harold Greenberg, Joan and Rick Morrison, Deb Crow, Peg Duffin, Jean Roughan, Wendy Codd, Diane Kennedy, Annika Woodman, Mary Jo Chadwick, Rita and Joseph Kaplo, Dottie and Mike Prakop, Cristin Zaimes, Donna Boudrow, Joanne Dillon Coyle, Betty Carney, Richard and Jo-Ann Goodridge, Marie Finn, Heather Vincenzi, Leonard Perkins, Kelly Nedeau, Roxy at Spectra's, Liz Pasek, Donna Winner, Meiliege Black at My Liege, Jane Sovich, Ellen Elliott, and Joan Carole Walker, Bill Sawyer—all of whom believe in me and give me encouragement and support and for the newfound friends that will come into my life as a result of this book's message.

To volunteers, the foot soldiers, who made all this possible back in the day: Peter P. Rice, Ronald G. Sutherland, Esq., Joan M. April, Deb Crapo, and Tom Dumais, and to the memory of Audrey J. Stomierosky.

Also, to those who helped during times when my back was against the wall: Brian Butler, Vice President of Newburyport 5 Cents Savings Bank, and Dr. Michael Rowan, Orthodontist, Newburyport, Massachusetts.

To my wonderful landlords, the Ross family—caring, hard-working, generous people.

To Maureen, a stranger who offered me her home in thunder and lightning storms while I was on my daily walks.

To doctors, dentists, nurses, staff, and the wonderful generous community outreach policies at Exeter Hospital, Exeter, New Hampshire, who kept me healthy through all my stress.

To Fr. Michael Griffin, former pastor of Our Lady of Miraculous Medal Catholic Parish, Hampton; Mother Angelica, Eternal Word Television Network (EWTN); and Joshua: each of whom continually teach me that "prayer is the path where there is no path."

To my 7 A.M. friends, whose fellowship sustained me through all of this.

To my son, Michael W. Schwartz, whose authorship of *Ratarra: The Legend of Damian* was my inspiration for writing this book.

To my editor and project manager, Linda Chestney of Nicolin Fields Publishing, Inc., who has been an excellent sounding board for me and has been able to smooth out my rough edges, and who wishes she knew me earlier and had a book like this when she was looking at colleges for her children.

To my copy editor and graphic designer, Joyce Weston, who nails it right every time—clean, clear, direct, communicative, and aesthetic visuals for a passionate minimalist.

And, lastly, and most importantly to my immigrant "parents," my grand aunt Nell Crotty and her husband Patrick Feeney, who talked and walked the faith of our fathers.

FOREWORD

Wisdom Learned from Life's Experiences...

Neither parents nor students are ever fully prepared for the college scholarship scene. I found out first-hand how seriously we can underestimate the magnitude of the scholarship process. I learned the hard way how much energy, effort, and tenacity applying for college scholarships entails. I waited too long to begin the process. My hope is that anyone who reads this book will be able to get a jump start on this rite-of-passage process, do it in a timely manner, and be successful in obtaining scholarships for their college-bound children.

Simply stated: I was a teacher and a single parent. I had two children ready to go to college. *"How will I ever pay for college for two kids?"* I asked myself over and over. I had little more than a basic idea regarding where to start. I did not know where to search for scholarships, grants, and financial aid for my child. I had no concept of what year in high school this financial aid search should begin.

I repeatedly asked myself: *"Where should I search—the Internet, local sources, library, high school guidance counselor's office? Or maybe the university or other source organizations such as the Rotary? What forms did I need and when were they to be submitted? Did my child qualify for need-based financial aid or merit-based scholarship or both? Why/how does one college application differ from another?"* So many questions and hurdles need to be negotiated by students and their parents to get the correct answers to succeed and be awarded financial aid.

Too frequently this task is left to the last year in high school, often in the few months before graduation. As a result, many scholarships, grants, and financial aid awards are not discovered until it is far too late to apply. Professional and highly-paid college counselors are so often out of reach for so many.

The book you are holding in your hands will answer your questions and organize you well for your journey into the world of applying for financial aid, and, I am confident, will reveal so many areas that you never knew existed. I had no idea how my children and I could afford the out-of-state colleges my children wanted to attend. But I'm here to attest to having great success in the search for financial aid for my college-bound children.

Joan not only helped us find scholarships but, more importantly, empowered us to search for even more financial aid, once my children were in college. Because Joan knew the value of long-range planning for college, my children applied for scholarships when they were juniors in high school. This gave them a competitive edge on paying for their education.

It is my firm opinion that writing the scholarship letters, getting all the necessary documentation prepared beforehand, instructing my children on how to write their own letters, assisting me in writing a "Parent's Letter" for scholarships, and mastering the art of researching the financial-aid maze could only be accomplished with Joan Ryan's personal attention to the specific needs and goals of my children. I can state quite assuredly that, without Joan's valuable help, we would have paid far more for college than we did!

Joan taught my children how to assemble a portfolio that would best reflect their individual strengths. Each portfolio contained numerous sources for grants, scholarships, and so much more. She took a personal interest in all of us. As a result, the end package was unique to our situation and needs.

The best part in working with Joan was that she empowered my children and me to find financial help for college on our own—even after we moved to another state. Joan shared information willingly and without hesitation because she truly wanted to help my children in any way she could.

While it was disappointing for me to learn that, in some instances, we started too late for certain scholarships and awards, it's good for you to know with earlier help from Joan this would not have occurred. Thus, I urge all parents to begin the search for college financial help early on—junior high or middle school is *not* too early to start.

Again, I emphasize that searching for financial aid, scholarships, and awards is a confusing maze. Joan led my children and me to the end of this maze, and I am eternally grateful for her help!

Joan Ryan's knowledge and expertise guided us through the complicated task of finding and being awarded scholarships that ultimately made it possible for my daughter to attend Worcester Polytechnic Institute in Worcester, Massachusetts, and my son to attend Northeastern University in Boston, Massachusetts. Both graduated with honors and now hold successful positions in the workplace.

Without Joan's expertise my children would not have been able to attend their first-choice college on my single parent/teacher income. I highly recommend Joan and her book for parents and their students who are applying for college!

Catherine Wojtkun, MA Ed.
National Board Certified Teacher
U.S. Presidential Scholars Program
Distinguished Teachers Award
Gifted and Talented Consultant

The information in this book is your *third* option.

- Your first option is to pay cash for college.
- Your second option is to go into galactic debt.
- Your third option is the *Scholarship Matters* methodology.

INTRODUCTION
You Don't Know What You Don't Know

While lying on my blue recliner with a stack of scholarship application forms in my lap, I pick up the next one and think...

Yes, my father was in the U.S. Navy. Yes, he served during World War II. Oh my goodness, yes, he had duty on a U.S. Naval vessel—a vessel that had been torpedoed and repaired, and the crew saved by their captain under extremely dangerous conditions. Well, this is amazing. We have all the eligibility requirements needed for my daughter to apply for the American Legion's Descendants of the U. S. Navy Scholarship.

Okay, let's see... The deadline date isn't for two months. We have plenty of time to fill out the application form and required paperwork and get it off in the mail—time to spare.

JUMPING THROUGH THE HOOPS

The institutions, organizations, and foundations providing scholarship money require proof of any claim in the form of legal documentation. I had no DD 214s (my father's official military discharge papers) and no membership cards. I did not even have his birth or marriage certificate to prove he was my father.

I also found out that my own birth certificate—one that I had used without any problem in my state for 40 years—was not a legal one. *What!* So, after months of correspondence with the U.S. Navy and multiple city halls, we still did not have all the eligibility documents for the American Legion's

Descendants of the U.S. Navy Scholarship, and the deadline date passed. My daughter was unable to apply.

> *The gap between eligibility and proof (verification) is in being prepared.*

Reality check: Even though I was eligible, I could not prove my eligibility because I was not prepared. The gap between eligibility and proof (verification) is in being prepared.

The word *prepare* is Latin from *prae* meaning *before*, and *parare* meaning *get ready*. Get. Ready. Before.

Joan C. Ryan

A LETTER TO FAMILIES...
Good News, Bad News

Unless we are millionaires, we probably need financial assistance for our children's college years. The good news is you won't need to come up with all the money to send your child to school—the college and outside institutions can come up with most of it—provided you apply for admissions using my methodology.

The bad news is we do need preparation and planning—the earlier, the better. Unfortunately for many parents, reality and panic set in around the eleventh grade. The worst case scenario is to start thinking about getting help securing scholarships in April of the child's senior year—*not a good plan.* You can do it, but you'll be in much better shape financially—and emotionally—if you start much earlier!

There are hundreds of scholarships and educational opportunities available, but not many people bother to apply for them because they do not have proof of their eligibility requirements. We can have all the scholarship opportunities in the world, but if we do not have the eligibility documentation, what does it matter? We cannot even fill out the form, never mind submit it.

The way to acquire these eligibility documents is *one paper at a time.* If we are able to schedule in an hour a week on a regular basis—the time we might need for taking an at-home course—and begin this process when our oldest child is in middle school, we will be in great shape. Many varied opportunities will be offered to our family members, and we will be in a position to enjoy the journey. In addition to receiving scholarship money through these documents, we will have learned organizational skills that we can use for the rest of our lives.

REALITY CHECK

If you think you are all set financially for your child's educational journey and do not need to do any of this, please think again. People have been known to lose their health, their jobs, their spouse, their benefits, their 401k, pension plans, stocks, bonds, savings, and retirement accounts right smack in the middle of their child's high school years. *Be prepared*—it's a great backup insurance plan.

> *Be prepared—it's a great backup insurance plan.*

We can do this document-compiling project calmly, enjoyably, and with considerably less pressure when our child is younger—or we can wait until high school and hold on for dear life through an emotional roller coaster ride. Either way, we will be asked by our high school, town hall, college, university, companies, foundations, institutions, and the local, state, county, and federal government to produce these documents. Our choice is *when*.

THE GOAL

My hope is that parents, by following the process laid out in my book, will come to believe that colleges are like supermarkets—they all sell peanut butter: creamy, chunky, or freshly ground. When an American citizen walks into a supermarket, she is confident and in charge. Let's transfer this confidence and empowerment from the supermarket to the college market.

Joan Catherine Ryan

WELCOME TO SCHOLARSHIP MATTERS

EXPERIENCE, STRENGTH, AND HOPE

After the gut-wrenching experience of watching my two naturally bright and gifted sons receive no money for college (and subsequently enlist in the U.S. Air Force and the U.S. Marine Corps), I wanted a very different experience for my daughter.

As a single mother, I thought I had arrived. I was confident I had enough AT&T stocks to pay for my daughter to attend the University of New Hampshire. But, as it does for many people, the flip side of life showed up on my door step—breast cancer, spine surgery, meningitis, loss of my job of eleven years. All that money meant for college went toward keeping a roof over our heads and food on our table while I lay flat on my back, physically disabled.

IGNORANCE IS NOT BLISS

It was at this same time, during my daughter's high school junior year, that I learned how *not* to research scholarships. I learned about all the eligibility documentation that I did *not* have. I learned the critical importance of the phrase "deadline date." I learned that even the nicest experts and well-connected professionals cannot be held accountable to always do their jobs correctly.

It was during this time that I learned that I was not alone—that there were many parents who found the college application and private scholarship process a mystery. I made a decision to do my very best to help my daughter go to college. As a result of working with my daughter as a team, when her scholarship award ceremony was held at her high school, she received 15 outside private scholarships. She ultimately attended a private, four-year college in Wenham, Massachusetts, with all expenses paid.

From the time my first-born son entered the military, I was sharing with neighbors and parents how *not* to do what I had done. I was teaching them what worked. In this book, I am using my 20-plus years of knowledge and experience with the families that have come for help in my business as "The Scholarship Counselor." I want to broaden my audience and help the public at large by publishing this book.

This book will walk your family through three basic steps: 1) creating eligibility documents, 2) navigating college admission and financial-aid, and 3) obtaining educational and private scholarship money.

This book will equip your family members with a "backpack," outfitted for any obstacles. You may not be able to count on anybody else (federal/state/county/local governments, high schools, colleges, universities, scholarship foundations), but you will be able to count on yourself. And when you put your head down on your pillow each night, you can answer "yes" to the question, "Did I do everything that was in my control to do?"

PLAN, PLAN, PLAN

In these ever-changing times, a family planning an educational journey can feel quite powerless.

The federal, state, town, and county governments' educational and financial policies seem to be changing every week. Whether it is because so many people are unemployed, or because the tax base has plummeted, or because government priorities have shifted, government-supplied educational aid has become a victim of the "Department of Debt"—or, if you wish, the government of the debt, by the debt, and for the debt.

The law and policy last year may not be the law and policy this year. Rapid changes take place at all levels of government, as well as at private and public institutions. What the Admissions Officer of the college said last year may have just been changed by the Board of Trustees and is not valid any longer. We cannot count on anyone but ourselves for continued, constant, and reliable control.

But if I am of Italian descent and can prove it, no law can change that. If I am a resident of Hampton for ten years and can prove it, no law can change that. If I have a natural talent in music, no law can change that either. I am solid—no one can take any of me away from me, in spite of constantly changing rules and regulations.

TAKING CONTROL OF YOUR LIFE

So what is a family to do? You *do* have the power of controlling everything that is *you*. By going through this educational preparation process early, you will be positioning yourself to be eligible for many opportunities.

Many scholarship companies, counselors, coaches, and websites exist, and each has lists of thousands of names and addresses of scholarships for every imaginable reason. We can have all the scholarship applications in the world right now, in our lap, but if we cannot prove our eligibility with documentation, we cannot apply.

Doesn't it make sense to get all of our eligibility documentation in order first? *Of course it does.* Doing this takes time. We cannot begin this when our student is a junior in high school and expect a lot of success. The earlier we prepare, the more documentation we will have for more opportunities.

Having Step One completed by the time our student becomes a freshman in high school will place our family in an excellent position. And all the footwork and collecting of documents will now be behind us, finished!

Then we can focus on Step Two, college admissions acceptance and college financial aid. We'll avoid a roller coaster ride of emotionalism by setting up a concrete plan for campus tours, exams, and essays. We'll have a concrete plan to have our family's financial picture look more attractive to Alumni Circle than to Wall Street. Imagine having all our family college application packages completed and ready to be mailed the first week of September of our student's high school senior year!

Now we have a full year to focus on a year's worth of monthly deadline dates in requesting, applying, submitting, and recording outside private scholarship applications—and we'll hit the ground running.

How to Use This Book

First. Complete the work on the **Questionnaire** as early as you are able. Ideally, you should have the Step One work completed by the time your eldest child enters the ninth grade.

Second. Complete work on college preparation, browsing, shopping, applying, copying, recording, submitting, accepting, and thanking. Ideally, you should complete Step Two by September of your child's high school senior year.

Third. Work on "inside" and "outside" private scholarships. *Inside* scholarships are those private scholarships that are given to colleges and can only be awarded to students accepted by that specific college. *Outside* scholarships are those private scholarships that come from anybody, anyway, anyhow—they are for any student going to college. They come from barber shops, deodorant companies, milk companies, fire departments, police, Walmart, art associations, and so on.

Follow up, Follow Up, Follow Up

It is critical to note that the tasks requiring outside action most certainly require follow up, follow up, follow up! For instance, you, as a parent, have a copy of your child's transcript, but the college wants the official transcript—and that can only come from the high school. You, as the parent, have to call, e-mail, confirm, and verify with the high school guidance counselor that the school has, indeed, submitted their part of the work—and then phone, e-mail, confirm, and verify with college admissions of each college that they have received all the official required paperwork from the high school. The lesson here is that a "100 percent *family*-completed package" is not necessarily a "100 percent *college*-completed package."

STEP THREE CONSIDERATIONS

Receiving the acceptance letters from the colleges as early as possible is important for insertion into the scholarship application packages—and of course, you'll only get that after you've done all the paperwork above.

If you focus early on Step Three, acquiring the names and addresses of outside private scholarship foundations whose deadline dates have not passed, you will lessen the stress later. The usual bulk of the local, private scholarship deadline dates is in March, April, and May of the senior year.

Step Three does not stop. When the student finishes applying for scholarships in the high school senior year, those awards pay toward only the college freshman tuition bill. Then he begins again. Every September through August while in college, the student will be working on Step Three to receive money each year. You need to apply for the money a year ahead of time to pay for the next year's college tuition.

A SPECIAL NOTE TO PARENTS STARTING LATE

Special note to parents addressing all of this late in the high school junior or senior year: Go through Step One and collect what you already have for documentation, make copies, and file them in your at-home box and in your student's accordion file box. (See details on organizing on page 100.)

Then, focus on Step Two, creating all the papers that make up the college application package. Find three colleges that are in competition with each other offering the same major that you want. Try to apply to each of these before the Early Decision or Early Action deadline dates run out.

Most colleges and universities adhere to rolling admission choices. You hear back within 60 days, but each college can have its own policy on responses. Get these "100 percent family-completed packages" out in the mail ASAP.

What do I mean by "100 percent family-completed"? It means that the family has done everything in their power to provide as much information as they are able. The family cannot supply confidential letters of recommendation. They cannot supply completed guidance forms. They cannot supply official transcripts or SAT scores. Although families can include *copies* of these papers, they are not considered official unless they are electronically sent in from the high school or have an official seal and stamp on the paper.

STEP 1

DOCUMENTATION

FILLING OUT YOUR QUESTIONNAIRE

Your Great-Aunt Edith, Fruit Loops,
and That Trip to Colorado—
Silent Sources of Money

The **Questionnaire** is the very foundation of the process for seeking out private scholarship information. Scholarships exist for everything!

So let's begin at the beginning. Our beginning in this process is filling out the Questionnaire as thoroughly as possible. Why? Because there are opportunities, educational benefits, and money for every single thing about every member of your family. Do not leave anyone out. Begin by answering questions about your immediate family and then answer the same questions for your grandparents and great-grandparents.

Scholarship opportunities abound in esoteric areas that you'd probably never think of—products you use, your family's heritage, your great-grandfather's military service, hobbies. All have the potential to provide scholarship money.

We will compile genealogical, medical, employment, educational, and other documents directly from our answers on this questionnaire. These documents are important, because one of the major problems for faculty and scholarship committee members is to weed out fraud. Our hard copy documentation will be the proof that separates us from the fraudulent. We will be legitimate.

We will be creating honest college and scholarship packages. Each document will verify and substantiate the next document, and the committee member scrutinizing countless applications will have comfort, confidence, and conviction in our information. We will lay all our cards on the table; the documentation proof will be right there. Let's begin.

(The Questionnaire is included for reference at the end of this chapter but can also be printed from the PDF on the CD-ROM.)

1   IDENTITY

Student's Name: Be careful to keep the student's name the same throughout the application. Do not change it from John B. Smith to J. B. Smith or J. Bernard Smith, and do not use nicknames. When an agency or institution has you associated with one name—and that name is linked to money or school programs—you want to be found.

Date of Birth: Some institutions will have their software set up so in a MMDDYYYY format that requires you to include zeros before the month or day, such as "06.01.2013." Others will accept "6.1.13," and some will have you write out the date, such as "June 1, 2013." Do as they ask.

Gender: Some scholarships are gender specific.

Address: This refers to a full residence description—not a post office box. Be able to prove where you live and how long you have lived there. Remember to include your county.

Phone number: You may want to give out your mobile phone number rather than your land-line number—or vice versa. Decide your preference and then be consistent.

Email address: Choose a straightforward, clear, sane address that you will not want to change as an adult. Don't use silly email names, such as *deliciouskisses, party girl,* or *country-cowboy.* Avoid them. Best bet is to simply use your name. Continually changing your email address could mean losing an important contact. Keep it simple; keep it real.

2   COMMUNICATIONS (NEWSPAPER/ LOCAL MEDIA/INTERNET)

Enter your local newspaper: *Portsmouth Herald, Los Angeles Times,* whatever you read. Add your other daily media sources—like the *Wall Street Journal.* Include your local television news channel, such as Channel 22 Town Hall Meetings and major metropolitan stations. News organizations and cable outlets many times offer private scholarships to local residents.

You should also retain contact information for these media sources to reach them in the future should you garner a scholarship from, say, American Legion Girls State. Then you can submit a news release to the local media to ensure the student and organization are recognized.

3 HIGH SCHOOL EDUCATION

Current Grade: Keep a file about your student for each grade attended. Include class schedules, graded papers, school activities, journals, and so on.

Grade Point Average (GPA): Your GPA score is often valued by scholarship and college admission committees as more important than your SAT scores. Your GPA can show your motivation, persistence, study habits, and—more importantly—how you manage your time, since homework is a key factor and is done on your own time.

Time management skills are a key predictor in gauging the likelihood a student will graduate from college. Some students may receive a high SAT score but do not make it into their sophomore year because of time management deficiencies.

Obviously time management skills are tantamount. In high school, most students grow up in the same neighborhood with the same friends—everything was pretty structured and predictable. This all changes in the college setting—the courses and activities are a huge smorgasbord to select from, and many new college students have not yet developed the skills to set boundaries. They may have a hard time saying *no*. No longer present are the longtime friends to counsel them against bad judgments or the parents who saw to it that the student had eight hours of sleep and three meals a day.

Pneumonia and other related immune deficiency illnesses can put a freshman in his bed for days. A new college student may not respect that there are only 24 hours in the day and that he can't ignore his body's maintenance requirements. Once sick, all classroom and extracurricular activities come to a screeching halt. Short-term and long-term plans go out the window. Discouragement ensues. Students may think, *"what's the use of being tenacious?"* and fall into defeatism. Quitting college may be the result, followed by anger, resentment, and depression.

We can stave off this possibility by teaching and modeling for our children a *steady-as-you-go* lifestyle.

SAT I and SAT II: Take these tests to get a score and then forget about them and focus on your day-to-day homework. Create strong relationships with teachers/employers/pastors/tutors. You are not the sum total of an SAT score.

Find out your College Entrance Examination Board (CEEB) number and your main school contacts and their phone numbers for your **Frequently Asked Questions (FAQ Checklist).** (See more on the FAQ on page 83.)

> *Send thank-you notes after appointments.*

When you begin your dealings with high school officials, jot down their name, title, department, job description, phone number, and days and times available. Send thank-you notes after appointments.

4 FAMILY

Siblings' Names, Ages, Grades: Hopefully, you are the eldest student in your family. Everything you learn about your life and the process of applying for contests, educational programs, and college or scholarship money can be passed down to benefit your siblings. Your experience can be a template. Most of what your parents are doing for you can be copied to set up similar files for your brothers and sisters.

Ancestral Lineage: Ancestry is often a virtual gold mine for scholarship eligibility. Find out what countries your ancestors are from and then get the documentation to prove it. Obtaining documentation from foreign countries may take months, so plan ahead. It is well worth the time and effort to do this research.

5 MEDICAL CONDITIONS

Allergies, Asthma, Disabilities: Be specific with dates of onset and name of diagnosis. This documentation is obviously important for medical reasons, but also for educational programs. Collect data on your condition: keep a record of how often you go to the emergency room or doctor's office and what the doctor does and prescribes. Keep a record of your medicines and the receipts.

There are foundations that give out scholarship money solely to students with asthma, but they require proof of the condition and all related care. Also, students who have asthma and are in athletics need to document this condition. Contact your specialist and request a summary of this information and all receipts on an ongoing basis.

6 EMPLOYMENT

Parents need to ask their Human Resource department at work about Educational Benefits for Children of Employees. Find out how long you have to be an employee to be eligible for these benefits. Request the application forms for scholarships or other educational opportunities, even if your child is too young to qualify now. Become familiar with the eligibility requirements and the application questions. Copy the blank application and write up a rough draft of your answers.

Working ahead of deadline shows you have time management skills.

If you conclude it is worthwhile, position your child to have the eligibility requirements by the time they reach the right age. As soon as the time comes for your child to apply, request a current application and file prior to the deadline date. Do not procrastinate and submit your application at the very end. Working ahead of deadline shows you have time management skills. Time is of the essence—do not show that you rushed. That is a red flag.

7 EXTRACURRICULAR ACTIVITIES

Members of your family may be involved in many different activities—there may be scholarship opportunities in some of them. Record names, dates, places, and descriptions of each activity. Take photos.

8 FINANCES

Be gut-level honest with yourself especially where you fill in outgoing expenses—do not hide under the covers. Use real numbers. Request your annual FICO score report, scour for errors, and then correct. This is an opportunity to be a positive example for your children.

9 FOREIGN LANGUAGES

List all languages you speak. For example, if your Mom comes from Poland and you speak Polish at home, your first language would be: Polish, lifelong. Then you would list English as your secondary language. If you are taking French in school, you would list that as ongoing study in speaking, reading, and writing French. Three years of one foreign language are considered helpful.

10 HOBBIES

What hobbies are you already doing on a consistent basis? If you fish every year and love it and have been doing it for quite awhile, then you can join the Fish and Tackle Association and subscribe to a fishing magazine that gives out scholarships. Research all the companies that produce your fishing gear and see what they offer for educational opportunities. There are scholarships available for every kind of hobby from A to Z.

11 MILITARY

Begin with the service of your immediate family and work your way out to all members who have served in the military at home or abroad. Get documentation of their service.

12   ORGANIZATIONS

Parents, pull out your membership cards and paperwork from each organization in which you or your student are involved. Copy paperwork and contact list for each organization. Are membership dues up to date? Record the educational institutions that you have attended and look up possible benefits for children of alumni.

13   RELIGION

List your denomination: Christian, Protestant, Methodist, etc.

14   SPORTS

List your current sports and those played throughout the years, including your positions, such as *"outfielder, softball."*

15   TALENTS

If you do not believe you have any talents, list what other people in your family, neighborhood, school, or church have said about you, such as *"you have a gift for debating and singing."*

16   UNIONS

Begin listing unions from your immediate family and work your way out as far as you are able to all extended union family members, great-grandparents, etc.

17   VOLUNTEER ACTIVITIES

List any service to anyone, anywhere where you do not receive money. This includes internships.

● PDFs of the **The Questionnaire, FAQ Checklist, FAQ Sample List,** and **Hobbies Sample List** are available at www.JoanCRyan.com or on the CD-ROM at the back of this book.

THE QUESTIONNAIRE

1 Student Name _____
　　　　　　　　First　　　　　　　　　Middle　　　　　　　　Last

Date of Birth_____ Gender_____

Address _____
　　　　　　　Street　　　　City　　County　　　State　　　Zip

Phone Number_____ E-mail _____

2 Newspaper/Local Media/Internet_____

_____

3 High School_____ Current Grade_____

Grade Point Average (GPA)_____

Scholastic Achievement Tests (SAT I) _____ (SAT II) _____

4 Siblings _____
　　　　　　Name　　　　　　　　　　　　　　Age　　　Grade

_____

_____

Ancestral Lineage (Includes racial, ethnic, and national origin)
Mother's Parents, Grandparents, Great-GP Example: Italy, Sweden, Canada

_____

_____

_____

Father's Parents, Grandparents, Great-GP

_____

_____

_____

5 Allergies, Asthma, Disability, Other Medical Conditions

_____

6 Mother's Employment _____
　　　　　　　　　　　　Company　　Town/State　　　Occupation

Father's Employment _____
　　　　　　　　　　　Company　　Town/State　　　Occupation

Student's Employment_____
　　　　　　　　　　　Company　　Town/State　　　Occupation

7 Extracurricular Activities_____
　　　　　　　　　　　　　　Mother　　　　Father　　　　Student

8 Finances: Mother _____
Monthly Incoming Monies   Monthly Outgoing Monies   FICO Score

Father _____
Monthly Incoming Monies   Monthly Outgoing Monies   FICO Score

Student _____
Monthly Incoming Monies   Monthly Outgoing Monies   FICO Score

9 Foreign Languages _____
Mother   Father   Student

10 Hobbies _____

_____
Mother   Father   Student
(Examples: fishing, bowling, animals, cooking, handcrafts, scuba diving, computers, sewing, etc.)

11 Military (**Example** U. S. Navy   WW II   Submarine   Purple Heart)

Mother _____
Branch   Theatre   Unit   Medals/Awards

Father _____
Branch   Theatre   Unit   Medals/Awards

Student _____
Branch   Theatre   Unit   Medals/Awards

Grandparents _____
Branch   Theatre   Unit   Medals/Awards

Great-GP _____
Branch   Theatre   Unit   Medals/Awards

12 Organizations _____

_____
Mother   Father   Student   Grandparents   Great-GP

13 Religion _____
Denomination: Example: Christian, Protestant, Methodist

14 Sports _____
Mother   Father   Student   Grandparent

15 Talents _____
Mother   Father   Student   Grandparent
Examples: Drawing, Violin, Writing, Public Speaking, Theatre, Science, Math, Languages, Chess

16 Unions _____
International   National   Regional   State   Local

_____
Mother   Father   Student   Grandparents   Great-GP

17 Volunteer/Internships _____
Mother   Father   Student   Grandparents   Great-GP

Other _____

_____

Tools of the Trade

So what do you need to maximize this journey? Well, there are a number of items you'll need to assure the adventure will go smoothly.

After filling out the Questionnaire as thoroughly as possible, we need to make sure we have a safe, "private home" for our document collection—a place where they will not be moved again and again or have to share space with kitchen recipes, bills, or other unrelated paperwork.

To get started, we need to gather some basic organizational materials. Here's what you'll need:

- An empty filing cabinet or a cardboard banker's box.

- Hanging files and file folders with third-cut tabs. Don't even think of using fifth-cut tabs. Keep it very simple.

- A multifunction color printer, with scan and copy capability, that puts out a lot of copies. This will pay for itself in short order.

- Three grades of computer paper: one for photo-quality images, one premium grade, and one draft grade.

- A Sentry or other fire-safe box that is large enough for hanging file folders—or rent a safe deposit box at your bank.

- A weekly calendar that will have sufficient space for all your phone and correspondence entries—or use your smart phone's calendar feature.

Your Mission: Collecting Your Documents

You probably already have some of the residence, local media, and educational file documents. But some documents require a long time to obtain. The ancestral and military categories are right up front in the time line, because they take the longest to aquire. Put what you already have in each category in the file folders you've created, and then go back to the beginning to work on completing each category's required documents.

Think of this project as a personal class or course. Find a day in the week and a time in that day where you work solely on completing one category. Schedule this time right into your calendar, making documentation discovery and recovery a priority.

The categories checklist is meant to be a sample only. I hope that some of the entries will open our eyes to even more possibilities in your own family circle.

Place each checklist right inside the appropriate folder in your box, add the documents as we get them, and then check those items off the checklist. This file box will become our very best new friend and will serve us well for many years in many different circumstances.

THREE-TAB HOME FILE DOCUMENTS

The following documents are examples of items that can be stored in your cardboard banker's box. You'll want to create color-coded tabs—for instance, the left side tabs could be highlighted in blue.

LEFT TAB—Blue Marker
- Acceptance letters
- Ancestry papers
- Anticipated funds received
- Associations/Organizations
- Birth Certificate
- Boys/Girls State application
- Citizenship Papers
- Eligibility Check-off List
- Essays (Core/Slice/Graded)
- Expense Sheet

- Extracurricular Activities
- FAFSA/SAR
- Family photos/Thank-you sentence
- Financial Aid Award Letter
- 1st & 2nd Semester Incoming Money
- Frequently Asked Questions (FAQ)
- Graphic Design Collage
- Income Taxes
- Medical/Immunizations
- Military and ASVAB
- News or Media Articles
- Parents' Statements
- Personal Profile Paper
- Photographs (casual)
- Portfolio Contents (poems/short stories/art/ photography/dance)
- Profile Financial Form (CSS)
- Progress Notes with Photos
- PSAT/SAT I/SAT IIs/ACT/APs
- Recommendations
- Scholarships Applied For
- Scholarships Received
- Sports/Music/Art/Photos/Resume
- Stafford Loan Papers
- Transcripts/Test Scores
- Tuition Graph Paper
- Unusual or Special Circumstances
- Volunteer/Internships

CENTER TAB—Red Marker
   12 Monthly File Folders (used for deadline date info beginning with September of the school year)

RIGHT TAB—Green Marker
   (Enrolled College Only)
- Admissions office
- Advisors' names and phone number
- Bills
- Bursar
- Career information
- Co-op program

- Course schedule
- Financial Aid office
- Major department head info
- Study abroad

SAFE BOX COMMENTS

> *They provide two keys. Make sure to keep one securely stored off-site.*

Requesting, receiving, and safe-guarding documents is tedious work that we do not want to repeat. This is why we need a theft-proof, fire-proof, and flood-proof storage unit for these documents. Sentry fire-safe boxes have sizes large enough for hanging file folders. They provide two keys. Make sure to keep one securely stored off-site.

If you don't want to purchase a vault-like box, find out from your local bank the rental cost of a security box that will accommodate approximately a milk-crate of papers.

While we are placing documents in our storage unit—whether at home or in the bank—we create a **Safe Box Documents Contents List**. The original list goes inside the box. Update it each time you add a new document to the box.

● PDFs of the **Safe Box Documents Contents List, Safe Box Document Sample List, Supplies Needed,** and **Supplies Needed Checklist** are available at www.JoanCRyan.com or on the CD-ROM at the back of this book.

Eligibility Documents

Congratulations! After all your hard work setting up a file system and obtaining your eligibility-specific paperwork, your results are in!

There are scholarships, grants, and educational benefits for everything about every member of your family. Everything. Every answer you give on the Questionnaire qualifies you for scholarships in that area. Within the answers you gave to each question are clues to where you are can look for scholarships, grants, and educational opportunities. Now take your answers, record those in your eligibility checklist, and voila, you have your very own customized eligibility list.

Items to include on your list:

Your last name
Your mother's, grandmother's, great-grandmother's
    maiden names
Your town, county, state, nation
Your high school
Your age and gender
Your GPA and SAT scores
Your allergies, medical conditions, or disabilities
Your choice of college
Your parents' employment companies and their income
Your employment company and your income
Your foreign language
Your ancestry
Your parents' hobbies
Your hobbies
Your declared major/declared minor
Your family's military history
Your military history
Your parents' organizations
Your organizations
Your parents' colleges

Your religion
Your parents' sports
Your sports
Your talents
Your great-grandparent, grandparent, parent, and student
    unions
Your volunteer or internship jobs

● PDFs of the **Eligibility Documents Checklist** and **Eligibility Sample Category List** are available at www.JoanCRyan.com or on the CD-ROM at the back of this book.

RESIDENCE DOCUMENTS

Collect and store documents that prove you live at your current address and how long you've been there. You need proof that this abode is your primary residence. Paid utility bills, cancelled rent checks, and bank statements will help, as will a paid renter's insurance policy, home insurance policy, or car insurance.

REAL ESTATE PAPERS

- Deeds, taxes, mortgages, insurance, maintenance receipts
- Condo/apartment lease contracts, security deposit papers
- Driver's license, passport
- Dog, boating, fishing, or hunting license
- At-home business license

NONRESIDENT DOCUMENTS

If you own a second or third home, condo, or land, you need to produce your bill of sale, your mortgage papers, deeds, paid-up taxes, and rental income papers. If you owned property but sold it, get all those papers in order. If you own property out of the country, have your paperwork ready.

This information is needed for the CSS (College Scholarship Service) Financial Profile, which we'll discuss in Step Two. The CSS Financial Profile is an asset beast (more than six pages long) that is required by many educational institutions.

Residence Documents Sample List

- Deed
- Driver's license
- Home insurance papers

- Maintenance receipts
- Mortgage papers
- Passport
- Property tax bill
- Real estate papers
- Town water bill

Non-Residence Documents Sample List

- Deed
- Lease contract
- Maintenance check off lists and receipts
- Other property mortgage papers
- Other property tax bill
- Other property water/utility bill
- Real estate papers
- Rental, condo, commercial insurance papers
- Rental income
- Security deposit contracts and receipts

● PDFs of the **Residence Documents Checklist** and **Residence Document Sample List** are available at www.JoanCRyan.com or on the CD-ROM at the back of this book.

NEWS ARTICLES AND MEDIA DOCUMENTS

Have a family member who reads the local daily newspaper (whether physical or online), print or cut out articles about scholarships and other educational opportunities offered in your town and area community.

Save news stories/articles about family members over the years. Print out complete articles from online news sites. These articles may further substantiate other related documents.

Some articles to save, for example, would be if your son or daughter is chosen for Boys/Girls State events and returns with photos, stories, and awards. You'd want to phone local newspapers and ask to speak with the reporter who handles local community or education news and tell him about this news. We inform local news reporters about all events in which our family is involved. Do not wait.

When our son or daughter does volunteer work, we take a photo of the exterior building with the name of the company or organization and a photo of our child participating in the volunteer effort. Reporters are always looking for local student news. The reporter may want to schedule an interview at your home with your son or daughter and take a photo for the article.

> *We inform local news reporters about all events in which our family is involved.*

Student, remember to write a short essay to go along with the newspaper article copy so that two years down the road you won't have to try to remember specifics.

If you are an immigrant, phone the local newspaper to let them know when you receive your citizenship.

Ask family members for any articles about grandparents and great-grandparents. They may not have the article, but they certainly will remember that one was written about their relative—many news organizations have online archives of old articles.

News Articles/Media Sample List

- Associated Press newspaper articles
- Book publishing/reviews/interviews
- Cable town hall, school board meetings
- CDs
- DVDs
- Internet sites, articles, blogs, social networking
- Local newspaper articles
- Magazine articles
- Out of town newspaper articles
- Out of state newspaper articles
- Parish/church bulletin articles
- Radio station interviews/announcements
- School newspaper articles
- Television interviews

● PDFs of the **News Media Checklist** and **News Media Sample List** are available at www.JoanCRyan.com or on the CD-ROM at the back of this book.

EDUCATIONAL DOCUMENTS

W e begin with our youngest child requesting the end-of-year elementary and middle school official report card and then work our way up to each older student in our family. Homeschoolers need their yearly portfolio paperwork to be current. These are especially handy to have when your child enters a contest, but also if your family should move to a different school district.

If you have children in high school, request their high school transcript with the official seal. Each year of attendance should include scores from tests such as PSAT, SAT I/ SAT II, ACT, AP, and ASVAB.

Attending a community college during summer break is a good idea to boost confidence and scores in high school math, English, and science. Consider taking advanced subjects that may not be offered in the local high school. Upon completion, request an official transcript. Also take advantage of tutor programs, such as Sylvan Learning Service. It is one more way to reduce stress in an area where improvement would be beneficial. Make copies of any completed contracts.

Read your report cards and transcripts carefully. If you believe an error has occurred, make an appointment to meet with the school official in charge of the records. Be prepared to bring proof of your academic record, such as graded quizzes, tests, exams, homework assignments, independent projects, and essays.

Take advantage of tutor programs, such as Sylvan Learning Service.

It is very important to have your child's extracurricular activities recorded in these transcripts. After you and your child finish creating a Personal Profile Paper (see Step Two, page 115), bring this paper along with backup to your guidance department. For example, if you include in the paper that your child volunteered at ABC

Company all last summer, bring along a signed letter from the volunteer supervisor or company stating dates and job description. Ask your counselor to record this information in the *Extracurricular Activities* or *Other* section of the school's transcript. The counselor may agree to all or only some of your added information.

If your child has been coded with learning disabilities, be sure to request these reports.

The Personal Profile Paper is the 800-pound gorilla in the application package. Once in a while a scholarship foundation will allow us to submit only *their* application form and an official high school transcript. We need them to know the information that is on the Personal Profile Paper, but we are not allowed to include it. But—if we have most of this information recorded on the transcript, the scholarship foundation will get to read pertinent information that is from the Personal Profile Paper.

> *The Personal Profile Paper is the 800-pound gorilla.*

Now it is time for the parents to request their own official transcripts (see the Educational Documents Checklist) along with a request for the official graduating diploma or program certificate from the educational institution.

OBTAINING TRANSCRIPTS

Because of fraud, some educational institutions have set up a safeguard of authentic transcripts. When you copy your original official transcript, the letters C-O-P-Y may spread out across your transcript copy. This is fine. Not all people, institutions, companies, or foundations will require the original—a copy of the original will suffice.

Request more than one copy of the official transcripts. They should be sealed in an envelope from the specific institution and signed across the back flap. When you receive multiple official transcripts, only open one for your needs and safeguard the sealed ones for those institutions that specifically request an original official transcript.

After we have obtained our own transcripts and our children's transcripts, certificates, and tests results, we need to move on to our parents' and our spouse's parents' educational papers, which may include the benefits and policies for grandchildren of alumni.

WHY THE FAMILY'S EDUCATIONAL DOCUMENTS?

We have begun compiling documents for our youngest family member and have worked our way up to older and extended family members. Why is this necessary? Why can't I just stop with my immediate family?

Suppose in our heritage gathering information, we find out that we have Italian ancestry. There are dozens and dozens of different scholarships for Italians. Some of these scholarship applications require that we produce birth records, church records, or school records from our great-grandparent's village in Italy. If, for instance, we have a news article of our ancestor's cobbler shop with a photo of him in it, the National Italian American Foundation (NIAF) will love to see it and place it in their archives. It may be only because of our great-grandfather that we are eligible to apply for the scholarship.

If our great-grandmother was a telephone operator for Ma Bell (for you young 'uns, that was the phone company at the time), she probably belonged to a union. Her union contract may have explicitly stated that her descendants would be eligible to apply for educational scholarships. No one in our family since that time has been a union member. She may be our only proof of eligibility to be able to apply for a union scholarship.

There are educational scholarships that are specifically for English and German ancestors from World War II. They must have both heritages and be from that time period. If those ancestors' children went on to marry Asian and South American people, no problem. We may believe that we are ineligible for such scholarships only to find out that we have English and German ancestry in us from 1943 and that we do, indeed, qualify for this scholarship.

We are now detectives, and each document will unearth clues about our relatives that we never knew. A clue will lead us to another investigation that will yield another cluster of information.

● PDFs of the **Home Schooling Portfolio Sample** and **Educational Documents Checklist** are available at www.JoanCRyan.com or on the CD-ROM at the back of this book.

Family Documents

Okay, let's begin by obtaining our youngest child's official, long-form birth certificate from the city or town hall. We may already have the hospital birth certificate or a church certificate, but in many cases those are not legal documents (see below) and therefore may not be acceptable to scholarship organizations.

We then go on to the next older child and so forth until all children's eligibility documents are completed.

Next, we begin work on getting both parents' documents:

- Birth Certificates: official long form from city/town hall
- Marriage Certificate: official from city/town hall

By the time we have finished producing the children and parents documents, we are beginning to get the hang of this. The next file will be the Grandparents' file.

- Birth Certificates: official long-form from city/town hall
- Marriage Certificate: official from city/town hall
- Death Certificates: official from city/town hall

These are the three basic, bottom line documents of proof: birth, marriage, and death.

If we are unable to get *legal* birth certificates (sometimes city hall loses documentation—natural disasters, etc.), use hospital certificates, religious sacrament certificates, and family Bibles as your next best proof. Relatives may have a copy of our parents' certificates. Finally, time-dated correspondence letters may help in lieu of official paper work.

As an example, suppose an uncle serving in WWII received a dated letter from another member of the family announcing that Aunt Helen had given birth to a 7-pound baby girl at Exeter Hospital, and they are naming her Sadie. That could serve as proof of her birth. Or it could be a letter about a baptism or birthday party. There is more than one way to find this type of information.

When we share with the student's grandparents that these documents will really help their grandson get money to pay for his education, many grandparents are eager to take over this investigation. They totally fall in love with the genealogy detective job. They have the most history to recall, as well as photos, rumors, and gossip—all of which are necessary in this sleuthing task.

When we have completed compiling the documents, we need to begin creating a graph of our family tree. Ask if any relative has already done this and is willing to share. There are also many software-based genealogy programs and online resources available that can help.

THE STEPS TO TAKE

1. Keep a research journal with the date, place, phone number, and person you contacted for a document. Note which family member was the subject of the request and the results.

2. Create a list of original documents.

3. Start a family tree graph.

4. Collect old family photos, stories, news articles.

5. List and take photos of heirlooms, coins, stamps, family Bibles, etc.

Some grandparents find it fun to write about relatives—where they grew up and went to school, where they worked, who they married, and how many children they had. Ask if the relative served in the military, and if so, where, when, and how.

You might find out why you draw so well.

What was unique about this relative? There are all sorts of questions that can be asked. You might find out why you draw so well. You inherited that art gene from your great-great-grandfather who was an architect for the town.

Writing a paper on each family member is a lot of fun. Adding news articles, correspondence, and photos brings it together for posterity. Please remember to copy everything, and file it somewhere safe.

The earlier you begin this the more of a game you can make of it. Enjoy the journey.

Sample List of Family Documents

- Adoption papers
- Birth certificates: long-form official city/town hall
- Citizenship papers
- Copies of family Bible recordings
- Death certificates: official city/town hall
- Family tree graph on ancestral information
- Green card
- Marriage certificate: official city/town hall
- Native American Indian tribal papers

● PDFs of the **Family Documents Checklist** and **Family Document Sample List** are available at www.JoanCRyan.com or on the CD-ROM at the back of this book.

MEDICAL DOCUMENTS

Writing a **Family Medical History Resume** will help identify what documents we may need.

With regard to allergies and asthma, we need to show a record of doctor's office, hospital, or emergency room visits to treat our symptoms. These diagnostic reports, or a summary, should be recorded on the official letterhead of the facility and signed by the attending physician or an allergy specialist. Request these once a year and then copy and save.

Is our child developmentally disabled or coded for other disabilities? Obtain any reports, assessments, and evaluations related to this care.

We also need proof of sports injuries. Request doctor's office, hospital, or emergency room reports signed by the attending physician. These are helpful when we accompany them with our Obstacles Overcome Essay. (See Step Two, page 119.)

There is no central repository of vaccine records. It is the sole responsibility of parents to provide this documentation. Don't walk around assuming that your child's medical records are properly filed in the physician's office—that would be false expectations. CONFIRM. We need to request, copy, and save all our immunizations records.

When the child is a senior in high school, make an appointment with her physician to get proper protection for the international college environment that she will soon be entering. It will help to schedule the appointment in May or June of her senior year, because some of the vaccines will have to be given multiple times over a five- to six-week period. Make sure that tetanus is up to date.

It is very helpful to have all this completed before our child enters college. We want to give our child enough time to experience any side-effects while he is still at home.

● PDFs of the **Medical Documents Checklist, Medical Documents Sample List, Medical Vaccinations,** and **Medical History Information Resume** are available at www.JoanCRyan.com or on the CD-rom.

Extracurricular Activities

Anything you do outside of the classroom is usually considered an extracurricular activity.

Take your time and explore life. One year you may try your hand at graphic design but stop that and start up something else the next year. Explore many different avenues. Try on a lot of different hats and when you find an activity that you absolutely love, do it with your whole heart and soul.

Try on a lot of different hats.

Whatever you decide to do, it is helpful to have photos of yourself engaging in that activity. Create a resume about it. Request letters of recommendation from people in an industry for which you have volunteered or taken a class. Speak with your local community news reporter to see if your activity is something that could be profiled in an upcoming article.

Employment is considered an extracurricular activity.

Don't forget—employment is considered an extracurricular activity. When you get along into your junior and senior years, try to have your activities reflect paid or unpaid internships.

● PDFs of the **Extracurricular Checklist** and **Extracurricular Sample List** are available at www.JoanCRyan.com or on the CD-ROM at the back of this book.

Financial Documents

Facing your financial reality may be temporarily painful, but lollygagging in financial La La Land is not only permanently painful, it can be harmful to us and those around us. Crunching numbers requires gut-level honesty. We get out of our heads and cut right to the core.

Getting Started

To start, get a pencil and two sheets of paper and handwrite a title on each sheet: **Incoming** and **Outgoing**. (See sample on page 47–48.) Why handwrite? Typing in the numbers on our computer can be a heady experience, but when we write the exact same information by hand, we get an almost visceral connection with our gut. Here we are connected with our own *truth.*

Then, for further clarity, subdivide that information into categories; i.e., home expenses, education, car expenses, and so on. You will be able to see where most of your paycheck is going and where spending may be out of balance.

After we have completed that exercise and have the outcomes for both sheets of paper, we need to sleep on it. Next day, refreshed and back in the hard reality of life, we set about another honesty exercise—determining what our priorities are—what is *needed* versus what is *wanted.* We might end up with three columns: Our Needs, Our Wants, and Our Desires. (But it is truly amazing what we can live without, once we determine a short-term goal or a long-term goal.)

If we are married, we should perform this exercise together with our spouse, if possible.

> *It is truly amazing what we can live without, once we determine a short-term goal or a long-term goal.*

After the both of us agree on the *Our Needs* list, we should discuss the percentage of money that will go to education for our children. Keep in mind that retirement and savings goals always need to come before children's education.

When we have a realistic plan, we need to bring it before our professional financial planner or accountant (someone versed in *Alumni Drive* rather than *Wall Street*) and listen to their suggestions and comments. If we have been rigorously honest and true to our values, not much should change except for maybe a tax credit of which we were unaware.

We may need to change our schedule for tax preparation. Employers have to supply us with our W2s in February 1. Schedule an appointment with your accountant as early as possible when you have that form. The early bird gets the worm—and the money.

THE FAMILY BUSINESS MEETING

The next step, depending on the age of your child, is the family business meeting where together you and your spouse make an appointment with your child to sit down in a quiet room with no IPods, TV, cell phones, or other distractions. The conversation could go something like this:

> *Your mother and I are pleased to tell you that we have done our financial homework, and we will be able to contribute up to 10 percent of your freshman year tuition at college. That may come to $3,000. But the remainder of the cost may be over $27,000. You will need to begin to plan on how you are going to pay for that part.*

Even a five-year-old can add and subtract. What he needs to know is that education provides options—and options are good.

So, parents, you may be asking if you should make the number more than 10 percent. *Absolutely not.* As a matter of fact, in most cases I counsel parents to offer only 5 percent. Why? Because a college financial aid director will immediately subtract—right off the top—whatever a family says they are going to contribute. She reduces that figure from the student's college grant and scholarship and gives less.

Children can get almost all the money they need for an undergraduate college education with their own power of GPA—the *package* markets the student. Parents need to give as little as possible to their children for an undergraduate degree while they pack away as much money as possible for grad school (50 to 75 percent of tuition). In grad school, foreign students get most of the money. It is difficult for many American students to get even private scholarships for grad school.

Back to our parent/child meeting. It is important for you to have permanent markers and paper at this meeting and print those numbers out large and clear. You could print your contribution number and have your child print out his number. When the child says, *"Like, how am I supposed to come up with $27,000?"* you respond, *"Glad you asked, because there are so many ways."*

THE STUDENT'S RESPONSIBILITY

The very first principle you need to know is that *you* have the power. You are not powerless. Let's discuss areas that are worth money:

> *Grade point average.*
> *Grade point average.*
> *Grade point average.*

All school *is* is homework. Approach each subject in this way: *If I am studying how the heart pumps blood into the rest of my body, I need to read it, write it, speak it, draw it, and act it out.* Being the best student you can be each day is **your job.** Dress like it, speak like it, act like it, think like it, and believe it.

Every person has innate natural talents and gifts. These are worth a lot of money. Suppose your great-grandmother had a gift in music, and you inherited her musical talent. Take music courses every single year in school and during the summer. *"But I don't want to be a musi-*

> *Pay strict attention to this principle:* Music will pay for your biology degree.

cian, I want to be a biologist." Please pay strict attention to this principle: **Music will pay for your biology degree.**

Visualize a pair of railroad tracks. One track is your talent and the other track is what you study. They are both coming and going in the same direction. Your ability to play music is needed and wanted by colleges. After they choose the crème de la crème from the pile of applications, they have filled only a few of their classroom seats. They still have 2,000 more seats, and they are looking for painters, pianists, computer hackers, debaters, writers, actors, animal handlers, mathematicians, dancers, singers, and so on. You get the point.

There are, of course, federal and state loans and grants for college, but these will not cover your costs. Most of your power and your money can come from private and college scholarships and grants—if you are *prepared*.

THE PARENTS' RESPONSIBILITY

Okay, let's begin... Every year request your free credit report, look for errors, and call and make corrections as needed. Your FICO score will be over 700, because you have moved from a La La Land budget into a reality budget and are practicing those principles in your life. Right?

Keep all your IRS tax reports on file. These help you create your employment resume.

Talk with your financial planner about college funding investments that are a safe option.

College Financial Directors are not concerned with your half-million-dollar retirement/401k account—they are interested in how much you contribute each week or each month out of your paycheck. They are looking for an imbalance. If you earn $1000 a week and are contributing $700 a week into your retirement fund, this would be a red flag. They would see that contribution as indicative of someone who doesn't need that salary for daily living.

Free Application for Federal Student Aid (FAFSA)

In January of your student's high school junior year, file your income taxes and then go online and fill out your FAFSA.

Print your PIN number on three different pieces of paper and place them in three different spots throughout your home. If you lose your PIN number, it is a nightmare to get back into your account.

Student Aid Report (SAR)

This paper will come to you as a result of completing your FAFSA. It will have all of the 103+ questions and answers on one page. This page is very helpful in your college application package and your private scholarship application package. (See Step Two.)

Estimated Family Contribution (EFC) Number

This number is usually located at the top right of the SAR page. You want this number to be as low as possible. This is the number that college financial aid directors will take into consideration in calculating your financial aid award letter.

CSS Financial Profile

The College Scholarship Service (CSS) Financial Profile is an asset beast. Position yourself to look as good as possible on a paper being read and analyzed by a college financial aid director who is earning around $50,000 a year. Please do not demand that on your $125,000 salary you just cannot possibly pay for college. Always put your values first.

Go back to your budget, your **Needs** column. If you decide you no longer *need* the sailboat and the time-share in Las Vegas, you should think about these before your student goes into the 10th grade. Why before the 10th grade? Okay, your income taxes get processed in January of your child's 11th grade, but these numbers reflect your income during her total 10th grade. (Your child will be applying for college during the 11th grade tax season.) These are the financial papers that the financial aid director will be looking at. If you sell and submit the sale of property in her junior year, the director will be looking upon these numbers as increased income, and your EFC (Estimated Family Contribution) will go up.

Here are some of the papers you will need to prepare for your Financial Aid Award Letters:

- 1040 Income Tax papers: parents and student
- W-2 papers: parents and student
- Credit report: parents and student
- College Scholarship Service (CSS) Financial Profile
- FAFSA (Free Application for Federal Student Aid)
- SAR (Student Aid Report) which comes from FAFSA
- Complete cost of college for one year. (Expense Sheet)
- Anticipated funds paper
- Special/Unusual Circumstances paper
- College Financial Aid Award Letters (for comparison purposes)
- Federal Stafford Loan info (a *must* to receive private money)
- Bank names, addresses, and account numbers

OTHER PARENTAL FINANCIAL CONSIDERATIONS

Think long term. Being employed by a public, private, or parochial school, college, university, or vocational school may be a huge help in defraying the cost of your child's education in that institution. Instead of being an assistant manager in an insurance company, you could be an assistant manager in the financial aid or admissions office in a higher education facility.

Where is your paycheck going? Has your family decided that mom's paycheck will go to savings for all the kids to go to college? Maybe it will go even further if she is employed by an educational institution. Maybe the benefits will stretch even further if she is employed by her Alma Mater? These are ideas to think about because of the skyrocketing costs of college.

Having a job as a student is an excellent way to learn about incoming and outgoing funds. Ideally, as soon as a student earns money, a healthy habit of money awareness should begin. Start having family money meetings as soon as your child mows a lawn for a neighbor or cares for children or bags groceries at the local supermarket. Have your child write out her

Start having family money meetings as soon as your child mows a lawn.

incoming money—"$25 from child care; $15 from Aunt Carol for help with yard work." In another column have her write out her expenses for the day/week/month—"dance lessons; cell phone bill." Have her subtract her outgoing from her incoming. Will she have to get out the bright red marker? Or is she in the black? Show her how to make adjustments to her outgoing funds. Show her the consequences of not being honest with her incoming/outgoing budget paper. Remind her at the end of each pay day to do an incoming/outgoing budget inventory. Extend the lesson to a yearly budget inventory.

Teach her the economic pie chart in words she'll understand. Teach her to write down a short-term plan and a long-term plan for buying items that require saving over time. Teach her the difference between a priority that is necessary and an item that is *wanted* but not *needed*. Teach her to be a successful steward of her money. Ask her to prepare a report at the end of the month for you to look over. Have her take a bookkeeping/accounting class for beginners and have her write everything down by hand first and then type it into a computer program. Children do not want any financial surprises either.

> *Children do not want any financial surprises either.*

Some families come to me with a budget maintained on a software program such as Quicken. Credit card purchases, the mortgage payment, paychecks, and fees are processed by the computer. Almost invariably I have found that, in these cases, no one in the family is emotionally connected to the financial reality of their lives.

One family stays in reality this way: They use a white board to hold themselves accountable to the grocery budget of $435 a month. They write the number $435 at the top of the white board at the beginning of the month and then subtract from it each time they come home from food shopping. The result is recognition; the awareness is immediate. This method communicates respect for the family budget. It communicates in a timely manner if additional funds are going to be needed from some other area of the budget because of a birthday or because someone was ill. The handwritten word works for the whole family.

When we make decisions, we need to ask ourselves *"what is the price I will have to pay for this decision?"* There is a price for every decision. Next question to ourselves: *"Now that I know the price I will have to pay for this decision, am I willing to pay it?"*

FINANCIAL BUDGETING

The computer-typing experience is a very heady, from the neck up experience. But, the visceral act of writing words on paper encourages reality. Our *throne of truth* is not in our head but in our gut—our second brain. After we have subtracted our outgoing number from our incoming, we look at the bottom line number, and we own it. Math is math—there is very little that is not precise. If we do not like the bottom line number, what are we going to do about it? Our child will see that he needs to take action.

Why should I do this Incoming/Outgoing paper? Why should I then bother to put this information into a category format? Why do I have to be very specific and itemize my daughter's dance lessons, recitals, clothing, shoes, hair styles, photographs, DVDs, makeup, underwear, jewelry, and transportation? Because you will be asked to do just this by some scholarship foundations.

Parents, please do not co-sign anything. Why? Because you need to keep your credit score high and your credit options open. Parents who co-sign loans are responsible for those loans getting paid back, and if you co-sign, you run the risk

> *Parents, please do not co-sign anything.*

that your credit availability could close down. So when your car dies and you go to purchase a new vehicle for work, your credit limit may already be filled up. When you have an emergency with your home's water pipes or roof, you may have already used up your credit line by co-signing for your student's car and college courses. *Be a positive power of example.*

SAMPLE FINANCIAL BUDGET—AKA, THE INCOMING AND OUTGOING PAPER

Incoming

Monthly take-home pay

Rita	$ 3,720
Ralph	2,000
No other income from any other source.	
Total monthly income	$ 5,720

Outgoing

Monthly charitable donations

Church, community, personal	$ 200

Monthly home expenses

Mortgage	$ 562
Real Estate Taxes	410
Home Insurance	200
Furnace cleaning	10
Plowing	15
Roof replaced	500
Septic System cleaned	30
Subtotal home expenses	$ 1,727

Monthly automobile expenses

Car payment	$ 308
Car insurance	300
Registration, Inspection, License Renewal	36
Car maintenance	146
AAA membership for 3 cars	14
Gas for 3 cars	300
Subtotal auto expenses	$ 1,104

Monthly utility expenses

Electricity	$ 100
Well water	0
Gas: water heater and stove	80
Fuel oil	150
Land line phone	70
Verizon service	90
Cell phone track minutes	10
Internet	15
Subtotal utilities	$ 515

Monthly grocery expenses

Food	$ 800
Non-food items (toothpaste, toilet paper)	200
Subtotal grocery	$ 1,000

Monthly pharmacy expenses

Prescription drugs	$ 100
Non-prescription drugs (example Mucinex)	20
Subtotal pharmacy	$ 120

Monthly educational costs for son

College coach	$ 100
College course	100
Books	25
Clothes	100
Computer	120
Miscellaneous	120
Subtotal	$ 565

Monthly personal maintenance costs

Hairdresser/Barber	$ 33
Dry cleaner	40
Laundromat for extra large-capacity items	10
Subtotal	$ 83

Monthly entertainment costs

Movie rentals	$ 25
Eating out	25
Tapes/Books/CDs	10
Subtotal	$ 60

Monthly medical costs

Co-pay	$ 40
Subtotal	$ 40

Monthly dental costs

Co-pay	$ 10
Sub total	$ 10
Total outgoing	**$ 5,424**

Results:

Total incoming	$5,720
Total outgoing	$5,424
Left over per month	**$ 296**

A Few Words about Loans

Students who need money to pay for college and who are going to be applying to many private scholarship foundations need to have a **Federal Stafford Loan**—subsidized and unsubsidized. Most private foundations will not award scholarships to students who do not have a Federal Stafford Loan.

Our student should create a **college savings account** in his parents' names. Then, year after year, he should deposit what money he can: birthday money, Christmas gifts, work–study, summer job money, private scholarship money, unused Stafford Loan money, and graduation gifts.

When you graduate from college, you'll reduce your final balance substantially by withdrawing what you were able to save from your college savings account. It is much better to have a really low undergraduate loan (or, even better, a paid-off balance) if you are continuing on to graduate school. You want to save most of your Federal Stafford Loan amount for graduate school.

Students, do not take on credit card debt.

Students, do not take out private educational loans. Do not take on credit card debt. Universities and graduate schools do not want to admit students who have a heavy debt burden from their undergraduate degree and now in grad school will be incurring an even larger debt. Most importantly, employers do not want to hire graduating students with debt that reaches out into the galaxy! *Debt is slavery!* You cannot focus on either studying or working for an employer when your whole focus is your debt. You are not free—you are enslaved. This debt affects all of your life's decisions—being able to purchase a car, being able to rent an apartment, being able to buy a home or condo, being able to purchase furniture and appliances, being able to afford medical insurance, being able to get married and have children and begin a new life's journey for you and your loved ones—all of these decisions will feel the burden of debt.

Take note: If an original student loan contract has no forgiveness clause, student's loans still have to be paid in full, even if the student dies.

THE IMPORTANCE OF MONEY

We are focusing a lot on money here, but we cannot afford to allow our *total* focus in life to be money. That will not lead us into the abundance we're seeking. Usually, it will not even lead to financial stability.

This is not to say that money is not important. We deserve to be paid what we're worth. And we *will* be paid what we're worth when we believe we deserve to be. But often our plans fail when our primary consideration is money.

What do we really *want* to do? What do we feel *led* to do? What are our instincts telling us? What are we excited about doing? Seek to find a way to do that, without worrying about the money. Then consider the financial aspects. Set boundaries about what you need to be paid, but be reasonable. Expect to start at the bottom and work up. But if you feel excited about a job, go for it.

Is there something we truly don't want to do, something that goes against our grain, but we are trying to force ourselves into it "for the money"? Usually, that behavior backfires. It just doesn't work. We make ourselves miserable, and the money isn't worth it.

I have learned that when I am true to myself about work and what I need to be doing, the money will follow. Sometimes it's not as much as I want, but sometimes I'm pleasantly surprised and it's more than I expected. As long as I'm content, I have enough. Money is a consideration, but if we are seeking spiritual security and peace of mind, it cannot be our primary goal.

> *Today, I will make money a consideration, but I will not allow it to become my primary consideration. God, help me be true to myself and trust that the money will follow.*
>
> *— Author unknown*

BUDGETING YOUR TIME

Let's talk about **time management**. This is what separates the men from the boys—or the women from the girls.

Create a time budget for each day of the week. After two

weeks see what worked and what did not work. Then reset your time budget to become *time management.* There are students with galactic SAT scores who do not respect that there · are only 24 hours in one day and that we are human *beings*— not human *doers.* Some of these very intelligent students do not make it to their sophomore year because of poor time management. Learning and practicing to manage time needs to be done before we enter college.

Attending college can be similar to being served a smorgasbord of goodies. If we are not already grounded in honesty and reality about our limitations, we may overindulge, go overboard, and pay the price.

When you complete your time budget, put it to the test. How many hours do you have in each of these five categories: (1) Mental, (2) Physical, (3) Spiritual, (4) Emotional, and (5) Financial?

- **Mental** can include learning, studying, observing, or reading.

- **Physical** can include sports, nutrition, physical fitness, physical labor, or dance.

- **Spiritual** can be volunteering, mentoring, attending 12-step meetings, role modeling, and tutoring.

- **Emotional** can include spending time with friends and family, a day of rest, sleep, hugs, kisses, hobbies, bubble baths, spas, and so on.

- **Financial** can be doing the exercise of checking incoming and outgoing funds each week to stay in the black.

What does your time budget look like? Is each area of *you* being fed enough? Is there balance? All categories of mental, physical, spiritual, emotional, and financial get exercised by being involved in your church, temple, or mosque.

Is each area of you being fed enough?

When all areas have been recorded, practiced, lived, and reset, create pie charts for visuals of your beautifully lived life. You have just come into your own. Now you are no longer a "lemming," but an individual person. To acknowledge the flow of your life through this exercise, purchase a day planner to record the daily history of your life. Know that you are a walking, talking, positive power of example to everyone in your life.

TIME BUDGET SAMPLE

Monday	Hours
Shower and Dress	1.0
Breakfast	.5
Attend school	7.0
Travel time to and from school	.5
Homework	3.5
Music Lessons	1.0
Travel time to and from music lesson	.5
Supper with the family	1.0
TV	1.0
Sleep	8.0
Total time spent	**24.0**

● PDFs of the **Financial Documents Checklist** and **Financial Sample List** are available at www.JoanCRyan.com or on the CD-ROM at the back of this book.

FOREIGN LANGUAGE DOCUMENTS

If one or both parents speak a foreign language, it would be very beneficial to speak that language at home. Children will easily pick up English in the neighborhood and school while continually using the foreign language at home. They may select a third language to study in high school.

If your child is in a middle or high school where there is not a language program that the family is interested in, find a summer program or a weekend program for that language at a community college. There are many technical learning programs as well, such as Rosetta Stone®.

> *Children will easily pick up English in the neighborhood and school while continually using the foreign language at home.*

When able, apply for and receive a certificate stating your level of proficiency in reading, writing, understanding, speaking, and translating your chosen language.

Look up job matches in the languages. For example:

- Medicine, Law, Health and Human Services, Theology: Latin
- Business: Japanese, German, Chinese, Russian, Arabic
- Art: Italian, Spanish, French, German

● PDFs of the **Foreign Language Checklist** and **Foreign Language Sample List** are available at www.JoanCRyan.com or on the CD-ROM at the back of this book.

HOBBIES DOCUMENTS

Sometimes, when one of my clients turns in her Questionnaire, there are two sections left blank—Hobbies and Talents. When I ask the parent about hobbies, I am told that there just isn't any time for hobbies. "I am too busy. For years I've volunteered to supply the church with landscaping. I have to tend to my own vegetable gardening as well, and if that wasn't enough, I am taking a Beginner's Spanish class three nights a week."

This is the part where I show the Hobbies Sample List to the surprised parent and explain that volunteering, gardening, and educational courses are all hobbies. A hobby is something that someone does *not* because they *have* to do it, but because they *love* to do it. If we do woodworking projects, Lionel Train collecting, sculpting, dog handling, or collecting 19th century dolls, remember to document, photograph, and compile proof. If we've attended workshops to learn how to do this hobby and received a certificate, copy and save it. Save attendance receipts from workshops and seminars.

Whatever hobby we do year after year counts—no matter how infrequently we may do it. If we go camping and hiking for a week, but we go every year, we need to look into camping and hiking areas. For example, there are camping and hiking magazines that offer scholarships to their subscribers, but you need to have been a subscriber for a few years in order to qualify.

Everything that goes along with the hobby has potential for money as well. The company that produces our tent or makes our hiking shoes may offer scholarship money. Expand your options—you'd be surprised at what is out there. Just get out that hoe and start digging!

● PDFs of the **Hobbies Document Checklist** and **Hobbies Sample List** are available at www.JoanCRyan.com or on the CD-ROM at the back of this book.

MILITARY DOCUMENTS

Military documents could be a major undertaking to collect, but the payback could be extraordinary. Think of this as a marathon—not a sprint. It will take a great deal of time and tenacity to make this larger picture happen, but looking back it will be well worth it. The military area requires a lot of follow-up and patience. Here's how to do it.

Begin with getting the youngest person's paperwork. In high school this could be Civil Air Patrol (CAP) or Junior Reserve Officers' Training Corps (JROTC).

Parents, you need to request your DD214, in addition to any DD214s for any other relatives, even if they are not direct descendants. This is one area where aunts and uncles who served in the military count. These relatives do not need to be still living for you to obtain these documents. You do not need any signatures of family members, but it is helpful to offer as much information about the relative as possible, including full name, date of birth, and any information you have about the military service. Make your request to:

Military Records, DD Form 214
National Personnel Records Center
9700 Page Avenue
St. Louis, MO 63132-5295

By FAX: 314.538.4175
By email: nprcenter@stlouis.nara.gov
Note: email requests may take up to 4 months
to be answered

Provide the following information in your request:

- Full name of relative
- Mailing address of relative at time of induction, if known
- Social Security Number

- Service Number (if applicable)
- Branch of Service
- Approximate dates of service
- List type of information needed (i.e., DD214, medical records, etc.)
- If the request is for yourself, provide your signature on the request.

Note: You do not have to be blood-related to a veteran to receive educational benefits. Children or descendants of veterans, including legally adopted children (again, proof is required) are eligible for scholarships.

> *You do not have to be blood-related to a veteran to receive educational benefits.*

Create military resumes for each relative that served. Obtain proof of selective service status.

● PDFs of the **Military Documents Checklist, Military Sample List,** and **Military Personal History** are available at www.JoanCRyan.com or on the CD-ROM at the back of this book.

ORGANIZATIONS DOCUMENTS

Parents, there will be organizations that you will be *naturally* eligible to join, such as the Sons of Italy, Ancient Order of Hibernians, Polish, Scottish organizations, and so on. By virtue of their DNA, your ancestors who came from all over the world now allow you ancestral eligibility. Try to obtain your membership cards to the organizations at least three years before you think you need them. Read the policy and benefits *for children of members* of this organization, in addition to benefits for members.

If you go skiing every year, look up ski clubs, ski organizations, and ski areas—especially where you ski regularly. Read the policies and benefits *for children of members,* in addition to benefits for members. Look up all your ski equipment and clothing companies to see what they offer for scholarship money.

> *Look up all your ski equipment and clothing companies to see what they offer.*

Organizations will have a mission statement for you to read to see if their purpose is in harmony with you and your child. Find organizations that honor your values. Join those organizations, get your membership card, read their policy papers, and highlight what applies to you. Then copy both sides of your membership cards to use when you request scholarship and/or education application forms. Do this right away so you will know the exact requirements. Collect news articles about the organization.

● PDFs of the **Organizations Documents Sample List** and **Organizations Documents Checklist** are available at www.JoanCRyan.com or on the CD-ROM at the back of this book.

RELIGION DOCUMENTS

L AW NUMBER 1: Copy all religious membership cards and documents of your immediate family, grandparents and great-grandparents. For example, your grandfather may have been a member of the Knights of Columbus, and there may be a scholarship from the Knights for which you have eligibility. Record family members' history and life experiences in their faith.

Copy your baptism, confirmation, and marriage certificates. Begin with the youngest child in your home and work your way up to the eldest in your extended family. They may not be legal, but if your town/city hall burns down with all the records in it, your copies, along with hospital records, will become the *new* legal documentation.

Copy evidence of religious youth group participation. If your church or temple tracks your participation in religious school, ask them for a copy of that information.

Some faith-based scholarships may require that you not only are a *member* of your local religious affiliation, but also that you have been an *active participant* over the years. They may also require that the student is currently attending their private or parochial schools. Keep your records up to date and correct any errors along the way. Follow Law Number 1—copy everything!

Create a resume of activities in your religion: altar service, youth choir, volunteering.

Request letters of recommendation from religious clerics in your faith. Provide them with your "intro packet" (your Personal Profile Paper, essays, and transcripts). Save and copy any articles of activities in which you were involved.

Create a contact list with the names, titles, addresses, and phone numbers of your priest, minister, rabbi, or imam.

● PDFs of the **Religion Documents Checklist** and **Religion Sample List** are available at www.JoanCRyan.com or on the CD-ROM at the back of this book.

Sports Documents

It's no surprise that a lot of scholarship money is allocated to sports, and that it covers all kinds of sports—basketball, football, soccer, tennis, track, and so on. So if your child plays any sports, make a list of her coaches and athletic directors with their phone numbers and email addresses.

Gather all your child's information and prepare a list of questions and statements about your child. Then phone the athletic director for an appointment. Request a Sport Scholarship Prep Handout and Resource Book.

You may have questions about sports scholarships. *How do I get the coach/athletic director to be accountable for his statements to me? Who is her boss? Does he have a job description paper? What can I expect to receive in writing?* These questions and others are covered in *How to Win a Sports Scholarship* by Penny Hastings and Todd D. Caven. They offer some excellent tips on pursuing this avenue of scholarship support.

Create a portfolio, a collection of your child's sports journey and create a sports resume, including:

- athletic information
- academic information
- personal data
- sports background and references
- athletic awards and honors
- academic awards and honors
- sports camps attended
- sports employment
- community service

Collect ongoing letters of recommendation.

Collect news articles with photos, the name of newspaper, and date of article.

Get DVD copies of games from high school or other parents, or make your own movies of your child's game.

Do all the footwork you can to document your child's participation in a specific sport, but do not put all your eggs in the one basket. Do not walk around in La La Land believing that your child's sport is going to take care of all his college finances. You must

> *You must have a serious backup plan.*

have a serious backup plan. If you do thorough footwork in all the areas listed on the Questionnaire, you will be covered.

● PDFs of the **Sports Documents Checklist** and **Sports Sample List** are available at www.JoanCRyan.com or on the CD-ROM at the back of this book.

TALENTS

Everyone has innate gifts and talents. These God-given gifts can pay toward your child's college education year after year. For example, if your child has a gift playing the piano, find him an accredited private piano teacher—one who belongs to the Music Teachers National Association (MTNA). If he attends a private music school, it should be one that is accredited and held to the highest music educational standards. Why? Because this is an eligibility requirement of many scholarship organizations.

Around the time our students are entering their high school junior year, many want to quit the piano, dance, or art lessons that they've been taking for most of their young lives. But this is absolutely the *worst* time to stop these lessons. These subjects need to show up on their transcripts year after year, without interruption. If you *stop* taking lessons—especially in the very year you will be applying for some high school scholarships—you may not have the eligibility requirements.

If the student has been developing his natural talent on an ongoing basis, this will be his ticket to paying for college. Remember those railroad tracks—they are both going in the same direction. One side of the track is piano, and that will pay for the other side of the track, biology—or whatever you want to major in. Art, dance, math, science, and cooking fill in the tracks! Choose high school electives that parallel your desired major.

Teach your child when she is very young that her talent is her job, and she needs to develop it through education. This job will empower her and offer her more freedom of opportunity. Her job will be to practice the piano every day, take private lessons, perform in recitals, tutor other children, and give back what she has learned.

Ask her, *"What do you want to be when you grow up? A photographer for National Geographic?"* Okay, let's play the piano so we can get that photography job.

When a child begins to play piano (or participate in art,

dance, math, or science) and enter contests, the family will discover that continuity is very important. Continue the lessons—do not stop them for a couple of years so you can "find yourself." You must have continuity. Letters of recommendation from accredited teachers—who are members of accredited associations—are also mandated.

Now, while you are playing your piano, build a portfolio of this activity: DVDs, copies of letters of recommendation, certificates, and a volunteer resume with letters of recommendation from the head of the organization. Collect and copy newspaper articles about your piano playing, your volunteering, etc. Play the piano for your church, and get photos and letters of recommendation from clergy.

Keep doing this *year after year*, because there is contest money for this *year after year*, but if you are not prepared, you won't be a contestant.

Resume Sample

Training from _____ through _____
Professional performances
Summer auditions
Summer programs attended
Movies/photos
High school groups and activities
Master class participation
Volunteer community service
Background
Awards/honors
Camps attended
Related employment
References
    Letters of recommendation
    Performance/event schedules
    Newspaper articles
    CDs
    Portfolios

● PDFs of the **Talents Documents Checklist, Talents Performing Arts Sample Resume,** and **Talents Sample List** are available at www.Joan CRyan.com or on the CD-ROM at the back of this book.

UNION DOCUMENTS

Our young student may never have been a member of a union, but we can look to his parents and grandparents to see if they've belonged to unions. Then, look at your spouse's parents and grandparents. Their union contracts may well include *"educational benefits for grandchildren, great-grandchildren, or descendants of the member."*

> ### Union contracts may well include "benefits for grandchildren, great-grandchildren, or descendants of the member.

Many unions have five levels: international, national, regional, state, and local. Your union's state, regional, or national policy may not have a scholarship, but your local or international may. Check out all five levels.

Pull up the union contract and policy. Find your information in black and white—and as current as possible. Then copy and highlight the information that pertains to educational, vocational, and college scholarship benefits for:

- Children of members: living, retired, or deceased.
- Grandchildren of members: living, retired, or deceased.
- Great-grandchildren of members: living, retired, or deceased.

Please don't wait until your child is in high school—*act now*. Acquire the addresses and contact names for all five levels of the union. Request scholarship applications by phone, email, fax, or snail mail.

Request a current *local* scholarship application form with guidelines from your steward or health and human service benefits person. If possible, find out who applied and won the scholarship last year, and find out how they did it. This information may be in a company news article or a union communication, such as a newsletter available on their website. Consider what the union was looking for and how the student exemplified that requirement.

Understand that some of the information in the scholarship application forms may change over time. This happens when the union takes votes about new stipulations.

Read the scholarship eligibility requirements and highlight them. If your child is not now completely eligible, you have time to take steps to make her eligible. They may ask for an essay. A well-written essay takes time and many revisions.

When the time comes for your child to apply, you can request the current applications and give the specific information to your child for each level of the union—with plenty of time for him to do a good job.

● PDFs of the **Union Documents Checklist** and **Union Sample List** are available at www.JoanCRyan.com or on the CD-ROM at the back of this book.

VOLUNTEER WORK AND INTERNSHIPS

I f you've done volunteer work or worked as an intern, request letters of recommendation from your supervisor on company letterhead and have a photograph taken of you engaged in the work. Copy and save these letters and photos. Here are some suggested documents that will be helpful.

- Signed acceptance papers on company's letterhead
- Signed letter of recommendation from your supervisor
- A record of the volunteer or internship activity
- Newspaper articles about the activity
- Volunteer/internship resume

Be sure to volunteer or intern in a place where you would love to work or an activity you enjoy. Also consider paid internships and job shadowing.

● PDFs of the **Volunteer Document Checklist** and **Volunteer Samples List** are available at www.JoanCRyan.com or on the CD-ROM at the back of this book.

CRITICAL STUDENT INFORMATION

THE TIME LINE

They say, *Preparation is everything.* How true. Below is a reminder of what to do and when to do it, so you'll be totally prepared.

FOR 6TH, 7TH, AND 8TH GRADERS

Families need to begin to document their family ancestral and military history. In many instances, these two categories take the longest time to acquire documentation. (See Family Documents on page 34).

Students should shop through the many contests and activities relevant to grades 6–12. They can google the National Association of Secondary School Principals (NASSP) or the National Association of Student Councils (NASC). From there navigate to **Students Contests and Activities**. Beware of age appropriateness, and the deadline dates to *register* and *submit* material. Some contests offer money, but others do not. This is a good place to practice entering contests and a place to begin earning money for college.

FOR 9TH GRADERS

> *Students need to take the Subject SAT II at the end of the 9th grade.*

Students need to take the **Subject SAT II** at the end of the 9th grade. Princeton Review publicizes study books for each of the 25+ subject tests offered. If the student hasn't already, he needs to begin drafting a Personal Profile Paper. (See the PDF of a Sample Personal Profile Paper.)

Every August or September, when the new Students Contests and Activities information comes out (see above), he needs to go contest shopping.

FOR 10TH GRADERS

You would benefit by doing one **college browsing tour** each month. As soon as you finish a tour, it's a good idea to fill out a customized college grading paper: what we liked, what we did not like, advantages and disadvantages, first impressions, and so on. Fill out and date this paper *immediately* after each tour, while your impression is fresh. Save these papers.

Make sure you consider both private colleges and public universities. The current reality of high unemployment and a low tax base has caused the tuition at some state schools to rise. Some *public* universities are now more expensive than some *private* colleges. In addition, some private colleges with large endowments are able to give out more money to their students (inside private scholarships) making it affordable to go to their colleges. So, even though their overall price tags may be higher, you may find yourself able to better afford a private college than a public university.

In the 10th grade, take PSAT and another Subject SAT II.

THE SUMMER AFTER 10TH GRADE

Get moving on **letters of recommendation**. If you are planning to major in biology, for example, be sure to have your natural science and biology teachers write letters of recommendation. Any science camps, science volunteering work, or internships should result in letters of recommendation.

Send an introductory package to the teachers we have chosen for this task before we leave for summer vacation after the 10th grade. Present them with our Personal Profile Paper and core essay—papers that our guidance counselor may not provide. Write a cover note to each of the teachers of our prospective major, name our preferred colleges, and mention that we will be applying for college money. *Do not use the term "financial aid."* For some reason, people believe this means we will receive millions of dollars of federal aid. Use the word *money.* Many well-meaning people have a delusion that federal financial aid will solve all problems.

> *Do not use the term "financial aid."*

When these chosen teachers have all our information and advance notice, they then have plenty of time to write a thorough, well thought-out letter which should be ready for us and/or guidance the first week of school in our Junior year.

FOR 11TH GRADERS

Okay, Juniors—this is a busy year.

Take an SAT I and two Subject SAT IIs before July, before your senior year. Because your college application package will be completed during the junior year of high school, by the end of August, you need to have the results of *all* these tests in hand.

You'll want to do one **college shopping tour** per month up to January. Go over your college grading papers that you saved from your browsing tours last year. What are your priority criteria now? Create a short list of your favorite colleges from those papers. Next, interview the colleges on your new short list and participate in classroom sit-ins.

This is also a good time (usually before March) to apply for junior year exclusive scholarship opportunities, such as those through Discover Card, American Legion Oratorical Contest, Ayn Rand Essay Contest, and Boys/Girls State.

Students need to register for the National Foundation for the Advancement of the Arts Scholarship as early as possible in the junior year.

THE SUMMER AFTER 11TH GRADE

If we want to receive a large college scholarship/grant, we need to spend the summer working on a **College Application Package** with all the family provided information. Colleges really recognize our seriousness of purpose. Complete at least three college admission/financial aid rough draft applications (all typed) in June. Essays are important and take time—they must be written and rewritten.

Do second rough draft college applications in July, and do the final version at the beginning of August.

Also, in mid-August, students need to have their outside private scholarship lists ready to request applications. If the application forms are not available online, mail **Standard Request Letters** *the day after Labor Day.*

FOR 12TH GRADERS

In the first week of our student's senior year, either the student or parent needs to make an appointment with the student's guidance counselor. *Hand carry* to that meeting any *college-required* guidance and high school evaluation reports. These reports are sent by guidance to the colleges that require them (not all colleges do). We should also bring along our handwritten thank-you notes to the guidance counselors, teachers, and coaches who have helped us.

In that same first week, mail out (via certified mail at the post office) at least three family-completed college application packages for admission and financial aid. Print out our record-keeping check list, and start filling in each of the colleges to which we are applying and checking off attachments included for each specific college.

The Early Bird Gets the Worm

Some guidance counselors and teachers will mistakenly believe that we are doing all of this footwork too early—they have their own ideas about time lines. They will not know that our senior year will be very busy indeed, applying for dozens and dozens of private scholarships. Remember, they are not getting the college bill—we are! Think of applying for private scholarships as a self-employment part-time job. While other students have not even completed their college browsing, we are applying for scholarships. This is the *"early bird gets the worm"* principle in action.

In each month—September, October, November, December, January, and February—request, apply, and submit **national**, **regional**, and **state** scholarship forms. Some private scholarships are offered year-round. The majority of your **local** scholarships have deadline dates of March, April, and May.

Too many families simply miss the scholarship deadline dates because they are *waiting for other people* to process their requests. *We wait for no one.* We are getting the bill.

Give people as much time to produce requested paperwork as possible. If we have a deadline date of May 1, think of it as April 1, and make your request to the person by March 1. Ask them if they can fulfill your request in two weeks. If they say *yes* to you, record this information. If you do not receive the paperwork in two weeks and three days, phone the person and remind them that they told you they would have the paperwork to you in two weeks. Now they say that they just need three more days. Okay. If you don't receive the paperwork in three days, you show up on their doorstep and don't leave until you have the paperwork in hand. We need to hold people accountable and responsible, and the first person we hold accountable is ourselves. *We* are getting the bill.

There is no one who is going to look out for the student's interest more than the student and her parents.

There is no one who is going to look out for the student's interest more than the student and her parents.

FOR 1ST YEAR COLLEGE STUDENTS

Congratulations! You're in college and your first year is paid for. But you can't give up the process now—you have three more years of undergraduate school and then perhaps grad school still to pay for. Now it's time to convert your attention to ongoing scholarship applications.

Create at least three mini-packets, comprised of the Personal Profile Paper, your Core essay, and resume. Schedule days and times that you will work solely on applying to private scholarships—both inside and outside. This will soon become your new part-time job. (See Step Three.)

● A PDF of the **Standard Request Letter Sample** is available at www.JoanCRyan.com or on the CD-ROM at the back of this book.

THE MAGICAL, MYSTERY TOUR

I f you have ever been on a college tour, you know it can be a very emotional, overwhelming, and romantic event for a high school senior. Your decision-making process is all caught up with the mystery of the college experience. You hear about all the colleges that your friends are applying to, and it is both exciting and scary.

Think about going to a supermarket—something we've all done our whole life. We are very comfortable there and sure of our decisions about which markets to shop at. There is no anxiety, no exhilaration, and no insecurity—because we know what to expect.

Now, suppose you were from a very rural area of China and were suddenly jettisoned into a U.S. supermarket. You would be astounded—perhaps overwhelmed—by so much food right in front of you and so many different kinds of the same food to choose from. It could be a very emotional experience. This is how it is for many young students and some parents visiting colleges. In some instances, this is what the colleges want—they hope that the parents and students will wait until the last minute to do their college shopping and be filled with this emotion.

"JUST LOOKING, THANK YOU."

You can avoid being compromised in this way by doing everything earlier. Get used to the college tour by going early and often. The tour will become commonplace, and colleges will become like supermarkets in your mind.

When the student is in the 10th grade, the whole family needs to choose a college to do a *browsing* tour that month—and then do it again every month during your whole sophomore year. Begin with a college that is close to where you live, and then visit a variety of colleges: four-year liberal arts schools, business colleges, and art colleges. Mix up the trips.

Call ahead to Admissions and ask about a tour. You can make this a *social* event. There is no need to discuss college majors or careers or talk about what everybody else did in college—this is a time to just *take it all in.* The family discussion could be about eating in the college cafeteria, and what kind of ice cream you are going to order. Keep the event social and light-hearted. When the tour is over and you are all back in the car, have the student write up a paper about the tour experience. What was interesting about this college and what was not liked? Date the paper and file it away. For each college visit, the student should write what he thinks immediately after the tour.

> *Keep the event social and light-hearted.*

When the student goes back to high school a seed will have been planted about the attractiveness of the college life and the thought, *"Oh boy, I better pay more attention to my studies."* This experience can create an amazing turn-around for students—*C* students can become *B* students just through this action alone, because programs, degree requirements, job opportunities, and financial aid all become personalized.

Parents and students need to have regular appointments with their high school guidance counselor and college counselor and attend all the information sessions. Even though, with your early preparation, you will be way ahead of these information sessions, there is always something to be learned—the regulations for education are continually changing.

Keep in mind, colleges are somewhat like supermarkets—but the product they sell is *education.* And because they are like other marketplaces, they put up their finger to see which way the proverbial wind is blowing. One year they could be advertising wall-climbing rooms and the next year an indoor pool in every building. One year they find out that female students outnumber the males substantially, and therefore the girls are leaning toward colleges with higher male attendance.

What should be important is what you will actually *learn* at the school each year and what will you actually *know* after obtaining a Bachelor's degree. Would you pass a graduation test? Does the school even offer one to see the results of their teaching programs? Is there any proof that this institution has actually educated you? Would you be accepted into post-graduate degree programs? Did your $250,000 education net you a job that will allow you to pay off student loans, keep a roof (other than your parents') over your head, put food on your table, and pay transportation costs and medical care?

If you can tour and explore many different colleges for a long period of time, you will become comfortable in choosing the one just right for you. You will become savvy enough to discern the marketing hype. You may find out that colleges that had solid educational reputations for hundreds of years may be sliding by on just that— their old reputations. Shop competitively.

Shop competitively.

A Student's Perspective

The essay that follows gives you some insight into one student's experience going through the scholarship process. It is enlightening to read. The student is my daughter, Catherine.

Our Scholarship Application Experience

Statistically speaking, I should not have gone through a $100,000 four-year, private liberal arts college, and with only $12,000 in loans to repay. I should have stayed at home, worked at a nearby shopping center, and attended a community college, course by course, depending on my financial status of each semester. This was not what I had envisioned for myself. College was not just extended schooling—it was to be a full-time, life-changing experience. I wanted to move out of my home, travel, get involved, and be available for all the opportunities offered at college. This, however, would take plenty of work. I was the first person in my family to pursue college, and ingredients to my success were faith and dogged determination.

Every day my mother would ask me, *"Did you do all you could do today to get scholarship money for college?"* Every day I needed to be able to answer, *"Yes!"* I drove everyone crazy in this pursuit. Daily I visited the high school guidance department requesting any and all available scholarship applications. The secretaries kept telling me no applications would be available until February. The head of the guidance department told me I was not eligible for the Tylenol Scholarship, meaning that I did not have the GPA or SAT scores to compete with the nation's top scholars who really should be given the application. I literally took hold of his arms and said, *"You don't know my mother! Give me the application."* The guidance department proved to be bafflingly unhelpful in my pursuit to pay for schooling. I created a new motto in response to this: *"They're not getting the bill."* No one was going to be as invested in this process as I was, and I could not expect anyone to understand or appreciate my initiative and perseverance. I was the one who would be left with the college tuition bill.

I regularly visited with my guidance counselor to discuss possible occupations and what I wanted in a college. I used the computer program available to choose a few colleges, but the questions did not seem to pertain to how I chose my school. Did I want to live in a rural or urban environment? Over or under 20,000 students? Hockey or football teams? Not being satisfied with this method, my mother and I visited over thirteen schools and interviewed at several of them. My litmus test was, *"Do I want to wake up here every day for the next four years?"* At one school after another, the answer was, *"No."* None of the schools inspired me in both mind and soul. However, when I planted my feet on Gordon College's soil for the first time, I blurted out, *"This is it!"* I had complete serenity in knowing where I wanted to attend. Every facet of Gordon College was authentically pristine, and I found myself feeling like I was on an eagle's wings being lifted to new heights and able to see incredible beauty and promise.

To prepare the best application I could for both college acceptance and for scholarship monies, I would frequent the Writing Center with an essay to edit. I was eager to hear constructive criticism, knowing that pride and a bad attitude had the ability to hinder this life goal of a college education.

Life did not stop during this period. Not only were class work and extracurricular activities important, but students whom I had known all my life were having abortions, contracting sexually transmitted diseases, and getting strung out on drugs.

My family was again in turmoil because of my father repeatedly having my family subpoenaed and attending court sessions. We were also on the verge of losing our home due to financial strains. These sorts of challenges, however, were not new in my life, and I had mastered the art of putting one step in front of the other no matter which storm was in my path.

My transcripts were not impressive, but my willingness to go the extra mile and my optimistic view of life seemed to inspire people. I was willing to spend money to make it. I had to get on a train to New York City in a new dress and coat, just for a brief, and very competitive, interview. Little did I know that I would receive $18,000 from that organization throughout the college years.

Rejection was commonplace. There were three frequent options in response to the scholarship applications I submitted: 1) the mailbox would be empty; 2) there would be letters from organizations stating that, in some way, I was ineligible for their monies—or 3) there would be outright rejection notices. Rarely was there an award letter. On Award Night at my high school, however, I was called to the podium fifteen times to receive scholarships from organizations at all levels—private, statewide, and national foundations—much to the shock of the guidance department, I am sure.

WHAT WE LEARNED

1. Time is of the essence.

  a. In preparation for eligibility of scholarships: Get involved in a sport, club, team, or outside organization early and commit to it for more than one year. For $12 a year, I became a member of my local American Legion Auxiliary and, therefore, became eligible for their scholarships. I received thousands of dollars on the town, state, and national levels of the Auxiliary and continue to give back to it through membership and involvement.

  b. Compile documents pertaining to yourself: Birth certificate, driver's license, proof of residence, proof of college acceptance, anything you have published or any articles in which you have been cited; general college essay, any and all recommendations from teachers, employers, teammates, etc.; proof of ethnicity, medical condition, or other characteristics relevant to scholarship requirements.

c. Be prepared for your scholarship application to get lost in the mail or for a delay in shipping due to holidays. Know that you may have received incorrect address information and your application is on its way back to your house to be sent out again—this could take a month!

2. *Copy everything!* Before and after completing a scholarship application, make at least one copy of both the original blank application and the entire completed packet. Typing errors, coffee spills, pizza stains, printer ink leaks, and misuse of space allotments on prefabricated application forms all contribute to its demise. ALWAYS have a copy of the original forms on which to practice: lengthen or shorten your answers depending on space available and visual appearance. After typing your answers, ask yourself if you would give money to this individual on the basis of this answer.

3. *Keep inquiring.* Keep searching for other answers, other routes, ask other people. *Utilize desperation!* If I had left the guidance office satisfied with their offer to call me when scholarship applications arrived, I would never have been as successful as I was in receiving local scholarship monies. If I had trusted the guidance department with all of my scholarship and college applications, the applications would have lost precious time sitting on a shelf waiting for the full shipment of those applications to go out in the mail sometime just before the deadline. I remember one very involved application packet I had given to the secretaries in the office to mail that day had still not been mailed a week later when I inquired about it! For college institution monies, timing is everything. The sooner the application lands on the Financial Aid Officer's desk, the more money will still be available and the sooner you will receive your award packet from that college with information critical to making your decision on which college you want to and can afford to attend.

4. *Community and extracurricular activities gave my personal profile life and interest.* Being academically capable is not

all that is required by most scholarship selection committees. Show them who you are and what you have contributed to your community. Have an official contact person for any unofficial volunteering activities you do so you will have a reference and proof of your activity.

5. *Market yourself.* You are trying to sell yourself and your dreams to an organization so these people will contribute to your college education. Make every packet shine. There is no room for grammatical, syntactical, spelling, or format errors, so do everything you have to do to make sure it is flawless in that regard. Type everything—including addresses on envelopes (not handwritten!). Encase your application in a plastic report cover. You never know which foundation will yield benefits, so put forth your best effort for even those scholarships you think are too small to matter as well as those which are so competitive you do not think you have a shot.

6. *Thank-you notes are essential.* Thank-you notes MUST be sent promptly after receiving any notification of award. This is not only proper in showing gratitude, but also sets you apart from hundreds of other applicants in the future, making you shine a little brighter the next time around.

7. *Follow all directions.* If somewhere on the application there is any limitation or requirement of documentation, obey it. For instance, if the statement exists, *"Do not attach any forms to the application,"* then do not even think about sending that whiz-bang of a recommendation along with this application. Or, if the statement exists, *"Please include a copy of your membership to the YWCA,"* then do so. A mistake in following directions will most likely send your application and all the effort you put into it down the drain.

8. *You make it happen!* No one will take care of your application like yourself. You are your first priority. Other than for perhaps your parents, this is true for no one else in the universe, including guidance counselors, postal employees, whoever is editing your drafts, and all others who may come in contact with your application on its way from you

to the selection committee. Ultimately, this is your responsibility.

You now have all the documents you need to start this whole
process each spring throughout your college years to maximize the funding available for your education. Create a file
while at school, so you may add the recommendations of your
professors, your college transcripts, examples of how you are
involved in edifying your college community, and new essays
relevant to the scholarship applications for which you become
eligible over the years.

Frequently Asked Questions, or "The Cheat Sheet"

This educational journey is rife with pitfalls, because we are entering an arena where we will be responsible for a blizzard of paperwork. We think we can't fail because everything is in our computer, right? Think again. Make hard copies. Make backup copies. Let us not break the First Commandment of Preparation: **Thou shalt not give away any piece of paper without copying it first.** Why? Because bureaucracies can lose things, and often do. We might think that because the people behind these bureaucracies have letters after their names that all our hard-to-obtain information will be efficiently processed. It's not necessarily so. We need to double-check on everything to assure that pieces don't fall through the cracks.

Please do yourself a favor—create a page called **Frequently Asked Questions** (FAQ). It will make your life so much easier. Check out the sample FAQ sheet on the website. It shows a list of questions for you to customize, fill in, and copy—on both sides if you prefer. Place your completed FAQ into a sheet protector and keep it right next to your computer. When information changes, be sure to update it.

When we do this preparation ahead of time, we are calm, cool, and collected. This makes a difference. When we are emotionally compromised, we cannot be getting down on our knees looking under our bed for shoe boxes with military information on our great-grandfather, grandma's list of prescriptions, or the union membership card identification number on our great-grandmother!

Instead of climbing up into the attic, diving into basement boxes, phoning or emailing relatives once again for an answer they've already given us three times, we just pick up our FAQ (or cheat sheet), and all our answers will be there.

We will be asked the same questions over and over again, and we will not remember the answers because, by this time, we are suffering information overload. So—just use this sheet, keep it current, and make your life easier!

● PDFs of the **FAQ Checklist** and **FAQ Sample List** are available at www.JoanCRyan.com or on the CD-ROM at the back of this book.

STEP TWO

COLLEGE ADMISSION AND FINANCIAL AID

THE WAY IT WORKS

Good going, gang! You've worked hard on accumulating documentation of your family's origins, your sports achievements, your volunteer efforts, and a myriad of other critical pieces of information. So now we are moving on to Step Two—the college admission and financial aid process.

Here are some guidelines:

1. Do not give away any piece of paper without copying it first.

2. Have faith, willingness, and persistence.

3. Trust—but verify.

3. Mom, dad, and student—be a team.

4. Honor your grandparents and great-grandparents— The Ancient Historians.

5. Do everything you can toward your goal—every day.

6. Be like Hallmark—"when you care enough to send the very best." Handwrite thank-you notes.

7. Put your core values first. Everything else will follow.

8. Don't make assumptions—they are the enemy of being a successful scholarship recipient.

9. Stand alone. Do not be a lemming.

10. The key to freedom and opportunities is accepting reality and taking positive action.

11. Be yourself; be real; be honest; do your best.

12. Wait for no one. (Remember, *you* are getting the bill.)

13. Try to complete most of the paperwork two months before the deadline date.

14. Colleges are big businesses that have lobbyists and agendas which are in conflict with federal government departments.

15. Federal government departments have lobbyists and agendas that are in conflict with the colleges' agendas.

16. Families have no lobbyists and must, therefore, advocate for themselves.

17. You are the customer. You are getting the bill.

18. A college is like a supermarket. A major is like peanut butter in a supermarket. All colleges sell peanut butter.

19. Browse, compare, cut out double coupons, shop for sales and clearances.

20. When all the lights are green, GO! (College acceptance, college program in major, enough money received from college scholarships, private scholarships, sports, performing arts, town, state, federal government—this is a match!)

21. You are the customer, act like one. You have the power. Use it!

22. The largest scholarship you want to receive needs to come from the college. Market yourself by creating a beautiful and interesting *college application package.*

You have the power. Use it!

23. Visualize your *college application package* as being worth $50,000 and treat it accordingly. (This guideline needs to be repeated again and again. Keep it in the forefront of your mind and on your fridge!)

THE ALMIGHTY COMMANDMENT: COPY EVERY PAGE

We touched upon this rule in Step One, but it bears repeating. To elaborate on the importance of this mandatory step, please read on.

This is **Law Number 1**: *Please,* do not give away any piece of paper without making a copy first.

While we live in an electronic, interconnected world, much of the process of scholarship application is still based on real paper. It is important that as soon as we get a document, we copy it twice. If it comes in color, copy it in color.

The original document goes into a safe box or a large Sentry or other fire-safe box (see Tools of the Trade, page 20). These documents could also be scanned and saved at an off-site location.

For our everyday needs, we set up a file using *copies* of our original document. *Please never work with an original document and never give away the original document.*

> *Never work with an original document.*

THE MASTER COPY AND THE GIVEAWAY COPY

Now we have two copies. The first copy is called the *master copy.* Place this copy in a sheet protector. This is the copy we use again and again to make copies for people, institutions, and companies that request them. It will always be crisp, because it is the first copy made from the original document.

The second copy made is called the *giveaway copy,* and it gets replaced right away as soon as one is given away. This way, when Company A requests a copy, there is one right there in our file, ready to go.

Once in a while, your original document will actually be a

copy. Say, for example, that a relative has an original document that you need, but he keeps the original and gives you a copy. Treat this as an original and follow the previously mentioned steps.

It is important to copy as close to the original document as possible. Copies that are copies of copies of copies will have print degradation that will get progressively worse.

APPLICATION FORMS

Every time an application is received, make a copy of it before it's filled out. This way, if an error is made or information changes by the time it goes in the mail, you have another clean, blank application to use.

Remember that you will be dealing with dozens and dozens of individuals and organizations over the course of this process. You will be responsible for many pieces of paper and will need to be highly organized.

IN THE DRIVER'S SEAT

Many women drive hard bargains in every area of their lives. Choosing shoes, clothing, makeup, hair styles, purchasing furniture, cars, homes, a cut of beef, meat markets, supermarkets, fish markets, sales, discounts, clearance items, coupons; all of these areas are scrutinized carefully by women.

How can they get the best for less? How will it help the environment? How will it enhance her spirituality? How will it harmonize with aesthetics? How can she get it conveniently? How can she get the best warranty, guarantee what a company offers, and on and on. These women drive hard bargains in every area of their lives *until* they reach the college door. Then it seems that our beautiful agile lioness turns into a lemming.

Unprepared emotions take over. Reason, logic, and sanity leave the building, and she is whisked away with the crowd of emotion-filled fanatics and victims. She loses her choice, her money, and her peace of mind—a high price to pay.

By going through this Step One, Two, and Three process, choosing, paying for, and enjoying college will be as simple as walking in the supermarket and choosing your favorite peanut butter. And, yes, the store accepts coupons in addition to the sale discount. To top it all off, the peanut butter sandwich tastes heavenly on your favorite bread with strawberry jam. *Delicious.*

You are the customer. College is just a business that wants to sell its product, which happens to be education. Just like supermarkets, colleges are advertising and selling the same product. Go after this like you would any other product.

CREATING YOUR OWN TIME LINE

Some guidance counselors, principals, and teachers have a preferred time line for the college application process for their high school seniors. They are thinking, *Let's do it this way and on our schedule so we can control the process, which will make it easy for us. Please—no individual family input, ideas, or plans.* For parents and students, the school plan collides and interferes directly with the family's success in obtaining scholarships.

Families who need and want to get private money to help pay for college have a date-sensitive window from September of the senior year until August just before attending college. *It takes a full year to apply to all the scholarships being offered.*

The family needs to work on all their college application packages in June, July, and August and mail their "family-completed" packages off to the colleges the first week in September of their high school senior year. (See The Time Line, page 69.)

This is not the time line that the school officials have in mind, but to be successful in your endeavor, it behooves you to work around their plans and execute your own time line.

It's necessary to do it this way because by September 1 of your senior year, you'll need to take off your "college-applying hat" and put on the "scholarship-applying hat." It's time to create the scholarship list, request scholarship applications, and prepare the private scholarship application packages for all the upcoming deadlines.

Some school officials do not care that money is needed for this college endeavor. For them, it's easier to tell you to just go take out a loan, or two loans, or three loans, but do not interfere with the time line they have set up in their school. Some have a plan for all the "lemmings" to follow in lockstep for a March and April process. Some do not know (nor do they want to) anything about all the work and months it takes to apply for private scholarship money—money that you do not have to pay back.

Why don't they care? Because... drum roll, please... *they are not getting the bill! You are.* The only people truly invested in doing what is right for us is *our family.*

School officials are hardworking people—and they have worked with a lot with families through the student's three years of high school, and they've been very helpful. Now, in the student's fourth year, there is a huge change. The child is now standing on her own two feet and preparing to leave the parents. She is deciding where to go to college, choosing a major, and figuring out how she is going to pay for it *all by herself!* She needs to wean herself from dependency on school officials at this point, because they no longer have a firm understanding of what is best for her. She needs to take the wheel.

LONGTIME REVERBERATIONS

My hope is that this book will open the reader's eyes to the long-term effects of the educational journey. We need to be aware of the new economic reality—soaring tuition, depleted state treasuries (which directly affect our public universities), and burdensome debt carried by college graduates. These realties affect every aspect of our lives—our marriages, our families, and the financial and educational decisions for the next generation. The exploitation of vulnerable populations by colleges needs to be addressed. They offer the dream of a college education by way of unprecedented loan contracts. Some employers (including the military and mission organizations) are privy to the personal debt of potential employees and use this information against the job applicant.

> *The new economic reality—soaring tuition, depleted state treasuries.*

We need to open our eyes to the possibility of a stark picture of life—an unfinished degree and decades of student loan payments. This reality must be seared into our minds. At what *real cost* will these decisions affect our lives? We need to revisit the question: *What are my core values?*

Educational loans are so well marketed that we are led to believe that this is the only way, the only choice we have, and we sign on the dotted line the same way we swipe a credit card through the machine—with no forethought. We have become passive lemmings thinking *"this way is less work,"* and we race forward with the crowds going over the cliff.

The benefits of a college education include that we become more employable—particularly during economic crises—than those with only a high school degree. We enjoy higher lifetime earnings and more career satisfaction. In the long run, a college education is one of the most effective investments a person can make, but it needs to be approached with one's eyes wide open.

Many colleges are hurting financially, which means they need us more than ever. This makes it a great time to college shop—it's the students who keep the college doors open. It is indeed a "buyer's market" on the college front.

The longest journey we make in life is from between our ears (La La Land) and down into our gut (our second brain, our throne of truth)—approximately 20 inches to reach our final destination of reality. So, onward and forward on our journey!

DON'T STOP DANCING...

Student, whatever you do, don't stop dancing, singing, drawing, painting, bowling, fishing, computing, sewing, knitting, debating, or cheerleading in your high school junior year, especially if you have been doing it year after year.

> *Don't stop dancing, singing, drawing, painting, bowling, fishing, computing, sewing, knitting, debating, or cheerleading.*

If you want to receive a Bachelor's degree in journalism, your ticket to a wonderful scholarship may be through one of your activities. In order to be eligible to apply for a scholarship based on that activity, you need to show a track record of proven interest, proven participation, and *current* participation. If you don't want to become a professional singer, that's okay, but your innate gift of singing can pay for your chemistry degree. You may have a paid ticket to a science education.

If you love the performing arts, but have serious doubts about ever becoming employed in that field, consider getting into a business program in your high school junior year and, like a railroad track, take your performing arts classes right alongside your business classes. Continue this railroad track plan through college, and you will be in very good shape for a multitude of employment options.

IN THE REAL WORLD

Parents, you and your student are your own best advocates in the human being to human being process. Keep communicating with people and understand that they are not mind readers. Help them understand what is going on with you, your spouse, your student, your finances, employment, and health. Life is ever changing, and people really need to know what changes have taken place. Health changes, job changes, marriage changes—they are all part of life.

Please share with each of your relatives your educational goals for your children and ask for this very special help while your children are still young, while the relative is still alive, while the relative is still speaking with you, and while he is able to remember important family facts.

It is always sad when a client comes back to me after trying to fulfill ancestral or military homework that I have assigned only to be told that they have tried everything, but they are stuck with unhelpful, uncooperative relatives.

Everyone's life is a journey of change—we are not the same person we were a year ago. Personal experiences have given us new insights and points of view. We are always learning new parts about ourselves that had not been revealed before. Every year—as if we are given a new prescription for our eyeglasses—we see the world in a whole different way.

If your student has terrible grades from the 9th and 10th grade but has turned a corner and now wants to participate in a positive way, address that right up front. Encourage her to write an essay about that.

If your student has terrible SAT scores, SO WHAT! Write about that right up front while everyone else is trying to hide it, or they retake these unreliable tests again and again to try for a higher score.

If your teenager commits a crime and is on probation, do not try to hide this. What an incredible life experience that does not have to be repeated. Have your teenager write about this experience. There isn't an adult alive who doesn't rejoice when a young person learns from a negative experience. Remember the Christian expression, "We are all broken," which expresses this sentiment so well.

HOLDING THEM ACCOUNTABLE

There is a saying, *Trust, but verify.* In this day, we have to not only verify, but also certify, substantiate, prove, validate, authenticate, corroborate, confirm, and follow up, follow up, follow up. When you are dealing with a person from a certain department, with a certain job title, and a certain job description, you expect this person to fulfill their job description. Please do not expect anything of the sort—some people do not do their job.

You must motivate them kindly—but hold them accountable. Like a child, when you ask them to do something (something they get *paid* for), you must help them in any way you can to accomplish this task. Say to them, *"What can I do to help you help me? I am willing to do anything."* And in the end, you phone them, you write them, you visit them, you e-mail them, and do everything you can to get them just to do their job. You are dealing with deadlines but no one else cares—just you. You care. So, as a last resort, you take your track record of proof of unfulfilled requests to this person's superior and deal with your deadline in person until you get results.

Your respect of deadline dates and making copies of all your paperwork will pay off, because sometimes the seemingly impossible shows up on your doorstep (like a postal strike or the entire Northeast National Electric Grid goes down as it did several years ago—to something less catastrophic like a request letter of recommendation from someone who just happens to be sailing the ocean on a four week cruise in the middle of the deadline date). You will be prepared.

Some of the nicest people in the world do not do their jobs. So this experience is painful. Reality is temporarily painful, but permanently rewarding. La La Land is permanently painful. Be grateful for the awareness.

YOU'RE STILL THE PARENT

Would you sit back and watch your 17-year-old purchase a $250,000 home? No, you wouldn't. Yet this is what some of the school professionals are telling you, the parent, to do. They feel that you should butt out.

If you were a college official and you knew darn well what your college's agenda was, wouldn't it be much easier to persuade an emotional 17-year-old than to work with his parents? If you were a private student loan company, wouldn't you be hindered in your aggressive pursuit of selling a loan to a student if she were taking advice from her parents?

Let's be clear. It's the student's responsibility to do as good a job as possible during the high school years so as to have the eligibility criteria that colleges are looking for.

The student, not the parent, needs to choose his major. It is up to the student to decide to choose a small college versus a large college; in the city versus in the country. These are very personal decisions for the student.

It is important for the *parents* to help the student ensure that the college is offering what it says it is offering in the major. It will not be the 17-year-old who holds the college accountable for the sales pitch—it will be the *other* adults. What if the college's Board of Trustees change the degree requirements right in the middle of your child's senior year, and the result would be that she won't be able to graduate from college with her class and accept that full-time employment position waiting for her? Hold people accountable for what their policy states. Does your child receive an actual *education* at the end of all this, or does she just know how to pass a wall-climbing exercise?

Hopefully, you have brought your child into the family college conversation by the 8th grade. Make them an important member of your family tribe. I used to say to my children, *"Because you are an important member of this family, I am going to allow you to take out the trash."* Or, do the dishes, or rake the yard. The family is a unit, a group, a tribe, a circle. Have the student become an *invested* member of the family.

> *Have the student become an invested member of the family.*

Have a family business meeting with a typed agenda every week. Discuss. Listen. Vote. Write up the notes and have your student type up the minutes of the meeting. Limit the meeting to a half hour. You will have lost the attention of your student if you go longer. Keep it simple. Keep it teachable, like this week's budget and decisions for the weekend.

Rather than throwing *money* at your children, give them *yourself.* Give them your power of example, your wisdom, and especially your honesty. Children can see right through lying parents. Our children are watching us. What are we showing them? When they look at our actions, what are they seeing? Parents can be everyday heroes if we try. We are lasting treasures for our children.

When the time comes to apply for college admission, parents need to bring to the table all their experience from hard-earned life lessons. Because I love my children, I am not going to allow them to get locked into a multi-hundred-thousand dollar contract with a large corporation (i.e., the college) without a lot of input.

> *The student is not the total sum of an SAT score.*

TEST SCORES ARE JUST PART OF THE EQUATION

A student is not the total sum of an SAT score. This is extremely important to absorb. Thousands of students have high SAT scores, and after a college has filled its quota on high scores, they go shopping for a violinist, an artist, an athlete, a dog trainer, a designer, and so on.

It's not necessary for students to keep taking test after test, just to get a higher and higher grade. The college people have a phrase for this: *Grade Grubber.*

If I have anything to say to parents it is to know your child and trust in the child's God-given gifts and talents. Do not veneer him to look different for a college administrator's criteria. Do not mold him into something he is not.

As a single mother, this concept was very important since financially, we lived well below the poverty line. So, I watched my eldest son, who was 10 at the time, and saw that he had a gift with computers. I gave him typing homework every day and paid him a small amount for each paper typed. With a small sum from Social Security ($1,500), I divided up the check to invest in my three children's gifts. I bought my son his first computer, printer, and software. At 13, he had his first paying computer job from a local businessman.

My second son was obviously a physical fitness lover, so I found a Karate school nearby and enrolled him there. He attended classes for years, receiving two black belts in Karate. As a new recruit in the U.S. Marine Corps, he was an instant leader.

My daughter, the youngest, was one with nature, animals, and the galaxy. I purchased a small-scale barn that was set up in our large back yard. We then proceeded to get a goat, sheep, rabbits, dogs, cats, and a chicken. She signed up for 4-H. She eventually became an awesome, unique middle school teacher.

Look at the whole child and see their mental, physical, emotional, and spiritual values. Do not starve one area to overfeed another area. Strive for balance. Make your investment on the insides of your child, not the outside. Nurture what is right in front of you.

THE KING-SIZED BED OR THE DINING ROOM TABLE?

Creating your college applications and scholarship packages will find you handling a blizzard of paperwork! What to do with all of it? Your king-sized bed and dining room table aren't options, because you need some place to sleep at night and a place to eat dinner—especially during the holidays. You'd have to move the papers often, and the more you move the paperwork, the more apt you are to loose something or make a mistake.

Having a *home* for everything lessens the stress. There is a place for everything, and everything in its place.

We covered the basics in Step One, Tools of the Trade, page 20, when we began to store our

> *Having a* home *for everything lessens the stress.*

documents. Now we're adding the enrolled college and private scholarship documents to the same box. Or, if you think it's easier, you can have a cardboard file box for the Questionnaire and documentation, plus another one for the college applications, and then a portable file box for the scholarship application process.

Now is the time to purchase a 24-slot sorter bin (or you can build your own). Staples has one that works very well and takes up little space.

One portable accordion cardboard suitcase box from Staples, Walmart, or other stores (19 Pocket Document Expanding Case File) works well. This box is for the student. It is portable and can be used in the dorm.

Mom and teenager should work like a team. Mom has her cardboard box and sorter bin at home, while her daughter has her portable accordian box in her dorm—both can communicate and function properly from their respective locations. This is especially helpful when mail comes in the student's name to the home. Mom needs to have permission to open it so she can keep her daughter at college up to date. Many times there is a deadline date involved, and Mom may not have the  time to snail mail or even FAX paperwork to her child. Also, by working together, if one is ill or incapacitated, the other team member can cover.

Constant communication, especially by email is very important. The student is too busy going to classes, studying for exams, and dealing with teenagedom to be on the phone with mom all the time. The written word works better. The student can print out the e-mail, follow the directions, and e-mail back to Mom who can do the same.

● A PDF of the **Sorter Bin Labeling** is available at www.JoanCRyan.com or on the CD-ROM at the back of this book.

THE INTRODUCTION PACKET

Many times throughout the student's educational journey, letters of recommendation will be needed. Say, for example, the student is majoring in biology. It will be important to select science teachers to write letters of recommendation. A form needs to be signed to allow sharing of the information, since the guidance department at the high school sends these letters under separate cover. What information about a student does guidance give to the recommender? If it is just a thumbnail sketch of your transcript, that doesn't begin to tell everything about you, does it?

One of the keys to success is to create an **Introduction Packet** about the student. This useful packet will introduce you to the recommender. But it can also be used for many other applications—contests, volunteer jobs, internships, employment, summer camps, extracurricular activity opportunities, college admission, and outside private scholarships.

> *One of the keys to success is to create an Introduction Packet.*

Enclosures in the Introduction Packet could include:

1. Personal Profile Paper with photo
2. Core essay
3. News articles
4. Unofficial transcript
5. Sports, music, and/or performing arts resume

Recommenders come in all shapes and sizes. A science teacher may know the student for just 45 minutes a day for a year, but a neighbor or dentist may have known all about the young person for many years. Other people who may be able to speak about your character include Boy or Girl Scout leaders, clergy, athletic or dance coaches, the veterinarian, your primary care physician, librarian, and 4-H Club leader.

There are two types of letters of recommendation: *closed* and *open*. You are free to request both. Write a cover note to your recommender addressing your desires.

> *I would love to attend Clark University's Summer Science Camp this coming July because I am planning to major in biology. I would appreciate your writing me a closed and/or open letter of recommendation toward this effort. I am enclosing information about myself to assist you in this endeavor. Please let me know if you have any questions. Gratefully, —*

Gather your request letter and enclosures and place this Introduction Packet into a 5 x 7 manila envelope. Also enclose a self-addressed stamped envelope (SASE). When you receive your letter of recommendation, make copies from the original and follow Law Number 1 (you know... copy, copy, copy).

Even if a recommendation letter will be *closed* and will be therefore sent under separate cover, the recommender still needs to know more about the student than the information the guidance department is apt to send. Send the Introduction Packet to those persons as well, and ask them to keep the recommendation letter in their computer hard drive, as you will be applying to perhaps 30 to 40 private scholarship foundations.

● PDFs of the **Recommendation (Open Letter of) Form** and **Sports News** are available at www.JoanCRyan.com or on the CD-ROM at the back of this book.

Who Is Your College Application Audience?

The readers of a college application all have one thing in common—they are made up of persons of academia. All of the people reading your college application have at least one college degree. They are all educated—college educated. They universally have an academic mind-set, which is focused on how the student will complement their specific college. Please meet some of your audience:

College Recruiters
College Admission Directors
College Financial Aid Directors
College Athletic Directors
College Department Chairs

College Browsing

Parents, you'll want to phone each college and schedule a 15 minute appointment with *each* of the above people during your college *browsing* footwork. Your child goes with you to the appointment, greets the person, offering a firm handshake, good eye contact, and a mention of his intended major. When you finish these appointments and arrive home, have your child handwrite a thank-you note to each of them.

Keep a **browsing/shopping journal** of their names, titles, departments, email addresses, and phone numbers. Make a note about the results of those meetings. It's a good idea at this point to create a **college poster board**.

College Shopping

Phone each college on your new *short* list and make appointments to meet for one half hour with *each* of the above persons during your college *shopping* phase. When you meet with them, remember the firm handshake, good eye contact—and a discussion about your selected major at their institution. Hand over a completed Introduction Packet with an enclosed cover note specifically addressed to each individual listed above.

Once again, when you finish all these appointments and arrive home, write a thank-you note to each of them. Go to your college browsing/shopping journal and add any new information from this round of meetings.

> *These positive actions have now convinced the faculty and staff of each selected college that you are a serious contender.*

All these positive actions have now convinced the faculty and staff of each selected college that you are a serious contender in becoming a student at their institution. They have placed your introduction paperwork in a file, and now, along with your packet information, they have the memory of a face, a handshake, and a smile to put with your name when you make future interview appointments.

● JPEGs of some sample **College Poster Boards** and the **College Poster Board Comparison** are available at www.JoanCRyan.com or on the CD-ROM at the back of this book.

THE COLLEGE ADMISSIONS APPLICATIONS PROCESS

Okay, student, you're now at the threshold of entering the collegiate gates—but only after you go through the admissions process. We're closer to the gate, so it will help to learn the lingo.

Early Decision

Binding: You apply before the deadline date (either the earlier Round 1 or the later Round 2) and, if accepted and *if enough money is given*, you *must* attend this college. You must notify all the other colleges to withdraw your application.

Non-Binding: You apply before the deadline date and, if accepted, you can change your mind.

Early Action

You apply before the deadline date (either the earlier Round 1 or the later Round 2) and if accepted, you can change your mind.

Rolling Admission

You are usually notified within 60 days of the college receiving your application.

Always read carefully what each college is offering in terms of admissions. Choose your match up offers with those colleges and fill out your **College Admission Matchup Checklist.**

A NOTE ON FRAUD AND COLLEGE ADMISSIONS

You would think that the largest problem that college admissions directors would have would be that too many students apply to their institution and that the largest problem for college financial aid directors would be not enough money for deserving families. In reality, one of the largest problems that both departments have is *fraud*.

For some families, applying to schools is so competitive that they will cheat to try to help their child. For instance, fathers or mothers will author the child's essays. In the financial realm, a divorced mother will submit her annual income tax information—without revealing to the college that she is living with someone who earns $100,000 a year.

Of course this backfires. The English professor is going to find out in a short amount of time how the student's writing abilities differ from his admissions essay. Some colleges will require an English and math assessment test on the first day—before the student is allowed in a particular level class. This fraud is very embarrassing and destructive to the student and costs the college time, money and, not the least, goodwill in the family's future interactions.

> *Fraud is very destructive to the student.*

This is precisely why a blizzard of documents are required at colleges, scholarship foundations, and governmental organizations. They have to weed out the lies from the truth. Years ago, we used just the FAFSA form, but college financial aid directors began to see fraud and disparity—a mother who earned only $20,000 a year but somehow had three homes, two sailboats, and property overseas. If relying on only FAFSA information, this mother was being evaluated for aid in the same way as a mother who was legitimately earning only $20,000 a year, renting an apartment, and holding no assets whatsoever. The **CSS Financial Profile** was created by the college professionals themselves so they could make more informed decisions when doling out their monies.

WHAT SHOULD YOUR COLLEGE APPLICATION PACKAGE LOOK LIKE?

First of all, the package needs to look like a 17-year-old student put it together—not a 45-year-old businessman. It needs to be *imperfect*. It needs to be youthful and colorful.

Why would a college give you money if you present an application in a $50 binder? This demonstrates that you can afford more than what is necessary. See the PDF of **Supplies Needed** from Step One for a *suggested* list of items.

The 5-pack multicolored report binders are neat, inexpensive, functional, efficient, and the perfect design for the college package. The front plastic cover is transparent to provide the perfect setting for the identification/cover page. Each report binder has a 100 sheet capacity, although in reality, 30 sheets is a better fit. The colors that these come in are black, blue, red, yellow, and green. If you want to match your cover sheet with the report binders, you can do that by purchasing assorted colors paper. It's fun to find out the college's colors, and then match them up with your college application package report cover and identification/cover sheet.

The paper that you use for text should also be reasonably priced, but the paper you use for your photo should be a quality glossy photo paper.

Double-side copies when you can to save paper. For example, the CSS/Profile, a six-page form, is best copied on both sides. But do not double-side essays. In fact, separate them with a news article or photos. Be frugal, but be kind to the reader by not using a font size smaller than 12 point.

Include in the package the one-page **Student Aid Report** (SAR), with 103+ questions condensed on one page.

All the papers on our **College Application Document Sample List** are very important, but we need to go back and remember why we are doing all this work. Why *are* we doing this? Because a college's number one admission's problem is *fraud*, and our package will be truthful. Each paper will substantiate and verify the next paper and so forth. An honest application package for admission? How refreshing!

THE COLLEGE APPLICATION DOCUMENTS

Print out the PDFs for **College Application Document Sample List** and **College Application Record Keeping Chart.**

1 Cover Sheet

See the directions on our PDF. Identify the college or university. Note whether you are applying for Early Decision, Early Action, or Rolling Admission.

2 College Application for Admission

Answer *all* questions—do not leave blanks or use N/A (non-applicable). If you have lengthy answers, type *"Please see Attachment A"* in the space and attach a separate sheet.

Staple the application fee check/on-line receipt/waiver onto the front page of the application. For the Common Application, fill it out and place here in your package.

3 College Application for Financial Aid

Some colleges do not use this form—phone financial aid to confirm. Add *"Application for College Financial Aid"* to your cover sheet. This is separate from federal or state monies.

4 Teacher/Guidance School Report Evaluation Form

Indicate if this form was sent under separate cover or sent electronically from the high school. Not all colleges require this.

5 Personal Profile Paper with Photograph

The Personal Profile Paper—your 800-pound gorilla—is discussed at length in the next chapter. Your photo should be a warm hello and friendly one that can be positioned on your personal profile paper.

6 Four Essays

Core Essay: a paper of persuasion, passion, and conviction about a subject or your intended major. Three paragraphs on one page; past, present, future.

Slice of Life Essay: a paper about an event that was important to you in your life.

Obstacle Overcome Essay: a paper with the key emphasis on the word *overcome*.

Graded Essay: an essay graded by your teacher.

No two essays should be placed back to back. Always separate essays with volunteer photos, news articles, or collages.

7   News Articles about You

Make sure you include the name of the newspaper and the date to your article.

8   Graphic Design Collage

"I Love My Major" greeting card or collage—any creative form of expression to show in a visual way what interests you.

9   The Academic Section

SAT I/II/ACT/AP/Community College Courses/Transcript: Include copies of all SAT/ACT reports, but communicate to the college that *official* reports have already been electronically sent to them. Include the date.

10   Letters of Recommendation

Include at least three letters, preferably from teachers in the subject in which you will major. Letters could also be from coaches, clergy, volunteer supervisor, and so on.

11   Sports, Art, Music, Other: Photos/Resume/ News Article/Media

When possible, use photos of you as an individual, rather than you within a team. For CD-ROMs, staple the envelope to a paper identifying content. Make copies of the CD for yourself.

12   College Scholarship Service (CSS) Financial Profile

Always include these multiple-page forms duplex-copied, even if the college does not request it.

13   Income Tax Papers (parents and student)

The first two pages (the 1040 signed copy) will suffice for this package. If the family has reams of supplemental forms, and the college requests them, you can mail these separately at a later date.

14 Free Application for Federal Student Aid (FAFSA)

Ideally, this should be filled out and submitted as early in January of the senior year as possible. (Remember to record your PIN number in at least three different locations in your home. Do not misplace this number.)

15 Student Aid Report (SAR)

After submitting your FAFSA, all 103 questions and your answers will be available to you in a computerized, one-page form called SAR. This report will give you your EFC number (Estimated Family Contribution). This important financial form gets placed in most of your scholarship packages.

16 College Expense Sheet

Admission committee members need to know that you have done your homework—that you realize the actual cost of attending a college for nine months out of the year, and that you did not rely solely on their institution's sticker price advertisement.

17 Special/Unusual Circumstance Paper

This paper needs to be written each year. Keep it to just one page. The paper should get right to the factual financial history of the parents' and student's life. Add medical or family situations that affect the likelihood of this student being able to return to college. Keep it to facts—not feelings.

18 DVDs/CDs/Slides/Portfolio Loose Contents

Attach a sheet of paper describing any separate information, such as The Fighting Scots Soccer Team versus The Haverhill Warriors Soccer Team Game of November 17:1 DVD, 1 CD.

19 Parent/Personal/Guardian/Mentor Statement Paper

After filling out many college application forms, you will realize that not all pertinent questions have been asked. Use this paper to offer the college information about the student that needs to be told—a slice of life, quality values the student portrays, an experience (obstacle overcome) that confirms courage or selflessness. Keep it short—one page only. This paper needs to be placed near the end of the package so that, after the committee has become acquainted with the student, they will put this information in its proper perspective.

20   *"I Love Your College"* Greeting Card or Statement

Numbers and statistics alone won't do it. Committees are looking for an emotional commitment to their college. They like their institution to be wanted, needed, and loved by a student and may even choose this student over one with higher GPA, SAT scores, or glowing activities.

21   Family Photograph with Thank-You Paper

Put a face on the people who are actually paying the bill, sacrificing many aspects of their lives so that this student can realize dreams and goals. It is, after all, not solely the student who will be involved with this institution for at least four years.

COMMENTS ON THE COLLEGE APPLICATION PACKAGE

Your teen may ask, *"Nobody else does the college application package like this, why do I have to?"*

Because to put it simply, *it works.* By creating your package this way, you are laying a foundation of truth and honesty, and upon that foundation, you will be creating a pile of papers that speak to each other. Each one will verify the next. Each one will substantiate the next. Layer upon layer will build the forthright story of your life, customized by you. This package reflects everything about you. *"This is your life..."* Your package is a presentation of *you*—mentally, physically, emotionally, spiritually, and financially.

You want your largest scholarship to come from the college you attend, so market yourself to create a beautiful and interesting college application package. Visualize this package as being worth $50,000 and treat it accordingly.

Imagine a long line of young men and women—each has

an application. Each is interested in the same result—they want to be accepted into the History Degree Program. They are standing in line, and at the head of line, there is a man behind a desk, collecting their applications.

This man can see the stains even when you submit them electronically.

Their white, wrinkled applications look pretty much alike, aside from some with pizza stains on them. (This man can see the stains even when you submit them electronically.)

Continue to imagine that all the young men and women in this long line have high SAT scores and transcripts off the chart. You consider your scores and transcript sort of average. You need to ask yourself, *"What can I do? How can I make myself stand out among all these men and women in line?"*

Distinguish Yourself

One of the surest ways to stand out is to create an application all about you. No one else is quite like you. You are a son, a brother, a nephew, and a cousin. You are a student, a neighbor, a parishioner, a newspaper boy. Show the man behind the desk who *you* are. Do not *tell* him—*show* him—about you. Imperfection is okay. Presenting ourselves flawlessly causes doubt, because we all cannot reach perfection.

What makes you different? Even though many of your friends at high school are ga ga over computers, you may like a different kind of machine. Maybe you take apart lawn mowers and put them back again—just because you know you can. You enjoy this and are considering a major in engineering. Okay, let's show the man behind the desk this part of you. Write a descriptive, one-page essay about the lawn mower. Make it a very personal love story. One paragraph on taking it apart, one paragraph on putting it back together, and one paragraph on how you feel when you are completing this labor of love. *"The 1-inch bolts crave to be aligned right up against the 3-inch gear, because that is where they perform their whirring chorus seamlessly."* Take some up-close photos of you taking apart the lawn mower and putting it back together again, and use them to make a collage on one piece of colored paper. Give your lawn mower a name.

Your SAT scores and transcripts are not the sum of who you are. Think of yourself like a diamond—a beautiful gem. All your gifts, talents, and unique experiences make up the gem's facets to produce a glitter when held to the light at a certain angle. No one else is like you. This is a great thing.

● The following PDFs for this chapter are available at www.JoanCRyan.com or on the CD-ROM at the back of this book.

ACT Report
College Admission Application Directions
College Admission Matchup Checklist, Choices, and Sample List
College Application Cover Sheet Directions
College Application Document Sample List
College Application Record Keeping Chart
College Financial Aid Application Directions
College Poster Boards and Comparison
CSS Financial Profile
Endicott College Application
Endicott College Financial Aid Application
FAFSA SAR Sent Note
High School Transcript Note
Identify Loose or Separate Items
Student Aid Report Sample
Teacher Guidance Evaluation Forms

PERSONAL PROFILE DOCUMENT

I repeat, the **Personal Profile Paper** is the 800-pound goril-la in the room. Parents, in your life and in your children's lives, there are situations where you need to present all of yourself—not just a limited, restricted, or politically correct version. Ideally, you want this document to be an *interview* paper. When you are unable to meet someone in person, this is the paper that they need to receive to stand in your stead.

Look at the PDF of the sample document of the Personal Profile Paper. You may customize the categories to your own life. This paper is very *fluid*—it will be changed again and again as your life changes.

It needs to be only one page. As information becomes out-dated it can be deleted, unless it is concurrent information, such as *"Future Farmers of America, school years 7, 8, 9, 10, 11."* But if you were a member of FFA for just the 8th grade and did not go back, delete that information.

Exhibit your life to the reader. What do you do in your life? What is important to you? How have you gone out of your way to belong to something in your life. Show this and be pre-pared to prove it. But be brief—no descriptions on this paper, please. Descriptions about specific categories are shown on different paperwork, such as your Arts or Sports Resume.

Your casual, friendly, warm color photo needs to be placed at the top in the center. A photo can tell a story of a thousand words. The whole personal profile final document needs to be on quality paper.

PERSONAL PROFILE PAPER DIRECTIONS

The people who will be evaluating your application will proba-bly never meet you in person (with the exception of the direc-tor of Admissions, of course). So, you need to help them *meet* you. You want your Personal Profile Paper to be as close to an interview as possible. This paper should contain information that is not included elsewhere.

Here are some guidelines on how to write this pivotal piece for your scholarship package.

1. Preparation is very helpful. If you know that you will be majoring in health and human sciences, you need to volunteer, work, and/or intern *directly* in the area of your major, such as a hospital, doctor's office, clinic or state welfare office, visiting nurses, Chamber of Commerce organizations, Lions Club, DARE, domestic abuse prevention, environmental protection agencies, etc.

2. Memberships show a *seriousness of purpose* and that you are actively participating in current informative areas. For example, if you are majoring in health and human sciences, you should consider joining the Junior Dentists Association.

   > *Memberships show a* seriousness of purpose.

   You are not just a mental and physical being, you are also a spiritual person. List the full name of your church, synagogue, or mosque under the Membership Category. But if you also did church work, that would go under the volunteer category.

3. Many students find the Leadership Position difficult to fulfill. What do you love? The environment? Okay, what specific concerns about the environment do you have? Recycling. Okay, does your high school, church, town hall, or recreation department need a recycling program put in place? You could do that and that would make you the *Founder of ABC Town Hall Recycling Program.* Don't do things you don't love—you will not do a good job! Remember, change is good. Every year you could love something different.

4. Employment should be in the area of your major if possible. The more time you actually spend in your major's environment, the more convinced you will be that you are doing the right thing; or conversely, and even more importantly,

you may decide you do *not* want a career of 8 to 10 hours a day in a particular environment. Then you can change your major and research other avenues.

5. Sports: list your position, *"Outfielder, Concord Girls' Softball."* Try not to be repetitious; just change the grades.

6. If the only place you have traveled to is Florida, list this, *"Walt Disney World, Orlando, Florida."* But if you have traveled to Europe, omit Florida. Instead, list the cities and countries of your travels; Dublin, Ireland; Valencia, Spain; Rome, Italy.

7. Some students may have a vast collection of poetry. They will need to include it in a separate category and list the titles, placing their most current poem first.

8. Music should be listed in as many areas as possible; Soloist, Piano for ABC Church or Community Center; Music Theory, Ear Training, Music History, and so on.

9. Languages spoken in the home should be listed first. Polish (Lifetime) and then the second language, English, and lastly any languages taken in high school.

● PDFs for **Personal Profile Document Sample List, A Student's Perspective, Kelley Coco, Personal Profile College Student Sample,** and **Personal Profile Sherry** are available at www.JoanCRyan.com or on the CD-ROM at the back of this book.

THE ESSAYS

Key essays should be included in the student application package. These are important pieces that will help you stand apart.

THE CORE ESSAY

The Core Essay reveals your passion about your major subject. Your enthusiasm should be captured in a one-page essay about when you first fell in love with your topic/major/subject, where you are now in your conviction, and where you see yourself in the future. This needs to be a love story. Three paragraphs are enough. Good writers or students of English will be able to communicate effectively on one page. More is not better.

A three-paragraph, one-page paper.
First paragraph on your past.
Second paragraph on your present.
Third paragraph on your future.

THE "SLICE OF LIFE" ESSAY

The second essay needs to show your readers a *slice* of your life—a snippet from some event that was important to you. Describe some small experience that had a large impact on your life, in three paragraphs, one page only.

An Example of the "Slice of Life" Essay

I entered the grocery store when an old neighbor of mine, whom I didn't like, was just leaving. I purchased my goods and left. While I was walking down our street, I saw up ahead the old man's grocery bag break open and everything fall out onto the sidewalk. Without my own permission, I ran up to help, picking up the can goods and putting them in my brown paper grocery bag.

I carried his groceries upstairs to his small apartment and as we emptied out the cans onto his kitchen table, he talked to me and expressed his gratitude, and he kept talking while I helped him put the cans away in his cupboards.

I left his apartment surprised that he was kind, interesting, and thankful. In my fear, I had completely misjudged him.

THE "OBSTACLE OVERCOME" ESSAY

If you have overcome an obstacle in your life, an essay about this would show more of who you are inside.

An Example of the Obstacle Overcome Essay

Nobody gets to choose the "life" cards they are dealt, but they do get to choose how they play them.

I was playing football for as long as I can remember and had excelled in this sport. My whole life revolved around being the top dog, champion, hero, celebrity, most valuable player. All my decisions and values, hopes and dreams were focused like a laser beam on football. When, at 17 I fell on the ice and injured my spine, had to have surgery, and was told that I could never play football again, I thought my life was over.

During my recovery, as each week passed, I noticed my parents still loved me and cared about me even though I was not now or ever going to be a football wonder. My friends became closer to me than I had realized and when we talked, we talked about real experiences in life that were important. Through months of daily physical therapy and agonizing physical fitness exercise, I was able to walk, bend, and stretch.

I met other sport enthusiasts whose athletic life was cut short by some accident or disease and they shared with me how they used this negative for a positive. Their personal stories opened my mind to all sorts of new possibilities and I received hope. Sports broadcaster, sports manager, sports physical therapist, sports counselor, sports medicine, or a football coach. Okay, I can do this and love it.

THE ESSAYS' PLACE IN YOUR PACKAGE

When you place your essays in the college package, do not place them back to back. Separate them by a photo of you volunteering or a news article or some other paper.

TALK TO YOUR AUDIENCE

It is important to remember that you will have two distinct audiences or readers.

From around October to January, during the Early Decision, Early Action, and Rolling Admission deadline dates, your essays' audience will be teachers, professors, faculty, and administrators of colleges, universities, and vocational schools. They are all educators, and therefore will be interested in your grammar, punctuation, and placement of your story line. How well do you express yourself? How well do you communicate your ideas, point of view, get your story across?

From February to August your essay audience will be different—scholarship foundation volunteers, in many cases. These volunteers will be from all walks of life, all religions, all different levels of education, and all political perspectives. Your essays should not offend anyone—they will be determining if you get the money. There will be plenty of opportunities in college to write controversial papers, but the scholarship application arena is not one of them.

> *Your essays should not offend anyone.*

The volunteers will not be as interested in the same areas as professional educators. This audience wants to know about you, *the person.* They want to meet *you* in this paper, so speak to them. Show them your insides. Remember that essays need to be a paper of persuasion, passion, and conviction. Move your audience to tears, laughter, or reflective thought. Caution: Do not claim victimhood. You will lose your audience.

These volunteers will be pouring through hundreds of applications. Three- and four-page, single-spaced essays will not be read, because the readers don't have the time. They are on the clock. They work all day long, go home to grab a bite to eat, and then speed out the door again to the meeting to select a candidate to receive their foundation's money.

> *Essays need to be a paper of persuasion, passion, and conviction.*

Write to express—not to impress. Less is more.

● PDFs for **Essay Document Sample List** and **Essay Document Checklist** are available at www.JoanCRyan.com or on the CD-ROM at the back of this book.

LOCAL NEWS ARTICLES

B e open to putting yourself "out there." That's hard if you're an introvert, but it's a role that we must play to get where we want to go. You'll get recognition in areas where you excel, and that recognition will often translate into media attention. But in the meantime, watch how others are doing this.

The potential for an article in the media might come along if you are chosen to attend Boys/Girls State events. If so, phone your local newspaper and ask to speak with the reporter for the local community or local education news. You or your parents should tell the reporter about your experience after you return. Be sure to take lots of photos, recall stories, and mention awards.

If you do volunteer work, have a photo taken of the exterior building with the name of the organization and a photo of you participating in the volunteer effort. Reporters are always looking for local student news. The reporter may schedule an interview with you and take a photo to accompany the article.

> *Reporters are always looking for local student news.*

Write up a short essay to go along with the newspaper clipping, so that two years down the road you will not have to recall specifics.

If you have just received your citizenship, phone the local newspaper. Ask family members for all news articles about grandparents and great-grandparents. They may not have the article, but they certainly will remember that one was written about their relative.

● PDFs of the **News Media Checklist,** two PDFs for **Leadership Extra-curricular, Leadership Extracurricular Letter Sample,** and **Leadership Letter of Recommendation** are available at www.JoanCRyan.com or on the CD-ROM at the back of this book.

"I Love My Major" Greeting Card

Okay. You're going to think this is ridiculous, but hang in there and hear me out. This is all about standing out in the crowd, and to do that, *we do what we have to do!* Here's a suggestion that has been very effective with the students I've worked with. It will make you rise above the competition. Will you actually carry it out? Your call.

Here's what you do. Let's say you are going to be majoring in nursing or the health care field. Visit a greeting card store and look in the *career* or *get well* sections. You can find numerous cards with all sorts of medical profession drawings. Use these to make a collage that expresses your love of your major and where you see yourself after receiving your college degree.

Be creative. Make a personalized collage that represents what is important about your college major, your personal life, or your family life. This paper could also represent a visual of your Personal Profile Paper.

You could set this up to be a performing arts collage, sports collage, or an art collage. Use your imagination.

Why a "I Love Your College" Greeting Card?

Visualize your readers sitting at a large conference table. Their mission is to separate the wheat from the chaff. They know the criteria for the college's acceptance requirements. They have read all the applications and placed them in piles. One pile has the same SAT scores, same transcripts, excellent letters of recommendation, and unusually good essays. Mentally, physically, and spiritually, each of these candidates fills the bill. They are the crème de la crème.

But they have 1,000 slots to fill. They move to the next pile to choose their missing oboe players, their football players, and their artists. How do they go about choosing from this pile of applicants whose qualifications could be very similar?

One way of doing this is to find out who has a deep emotional connection to their institution. Colleges have large egos. Administrators, faculty, and staff are prejudiced toward their institution—as they should be.

> *Administrators, faculty, and staff are prejudiced toward their institution—as they should be.*

Smart families have researched their teenager's number one choice (or top four choices) of colleges. They know the institution's history, outstanding accomplishments, unique philosophy, and mission statement. They know that this college has the student's chosen major and an amazing program in that major. This institution has planned out the various department's majors to be beneficial, practical, and user-friendly for the students.

Student, go card shopping as if you were purchasing this card for a boyfriend or girlfriend. It should be a very romantic card. Write on the inside of the card, *"To My Boston University"* or *"To My Salve Regina,"* and then underneath the romantic text, you write, *"I Love You, Boston University."* Sign, *"With all my love, Joan Ryan,"* and with double-sided tape, place this card on a paper to go into your package.

You can do this for all your top choice colleges, even though there is only one college that *really* has your heart.

● PDFs of the **Graphic Design Collage Sample** and **Romantic Greeting Card** are available at www.JoanCRyan.com or on the CD-ROM at the back of this book.

THE ACADEMIC SECTION

Make sure *ahead of time* that you have all the requirements to graduate from high school—not just the number of credits, but all the required courses. The high school's policy may be quite different from your own idea of this. *Confirm.*

SAT I, SAT II, AND ACT

All your SAT exams need to be completed and received by the summer after your high school junior year. It is during this summer time that you'll want to be packaging the attachments for each of your college choices.

When you receive the results of your SAT I and SAT II or ACT, print them in color. Be careful that the information at the very bottom is not cut off.

TRANSCRIPTS

Bring your Personal Profile Paper and extracurricular experiences to guidance. Request that the Personal Profile Paper's information be recorded on your transcript in the "Other Information" or "Other Activities" section. Guidance may accept some but not all information you present.

Unfortunately, because of so much fraud, most high schools will not give you an original transcript. These will have to be requested and sent under separate cover by the guidance department. If you are able to get your transcript, it will probably have the word "UNOFFICIAL" or "C-O-P-Y" stretched across the report. This is fine as long as you have a paper in the package that communicates to the reader that the *official* transcript has been sent under separate cover.

RECOMMENDATION LETTERS

High schools usually distribute a form to be filled out by the students to request letters of recommendation. Please make sure that you ask the teachers in the subject of your chosen major. For instance, if you are going to major in art at college, your first choices should be your art teacher and the head of the art department.

Then personally deliver to each of the teachers who are writing recommendations your Introduction Package (cover note, Personal Profile Paper, essay, transcript, news article, etc.). The information that guidance gives them may be incomplete, and you want them to know all about you so they can write a thorough, well thought-out letter. These letters are sometimes confidential (i.e., *closed*)—they may be sent to the colleges under separate cover. Please send a handwritten thank-you note to each of these teachers.

You need to ask other people in your life to recommend you as well—the supervisor of your volunteer activity, your doctor, dentist, clergy, or neighbor. Some of these people have known you your whole life, whereas a teacher may only know you for a school year or two. Also, a letter of recommendation from a peer is always a welcomed and cherished letter. If possible, have the letter written on the organization's letterhead.

SPORT, ART, OR MUSIC SECTION

Students, package up your high school experiences. Place photos in plastic sleeves with a paper identifying who, what, why, how, and when. Or provide a recent CD or DVD, and again, identify all these packets.

● PDFs of the **SAT Transcript ACT Samples, Community College Transcript Sample, High School Transcript Note, Recommendation Letters (3), Softball Resume, Performing Arts Resume,** and **CD Sample Page** are available at www.JoanCRyan.com or on the CD-ROM at the back of this book.

FINANCIAL SECTION OF THE COLLEGE APPLICATION

Parents, if you thought you had privacy, especially financial privacy, it ends with the college application process. The following documents will be needed.

- The **College Scholarship Service (CSS) Financial Profile** is the asset-beast paper that needs to be filled out and sent to all colleges—even those who do not ask for it. Put all your cards on the table—be open and honest. You can copy this multi-page form on both sides of the paper to get it as condensed as possible. The results of this paper can possibly become your very best new friend.

> *If you thought you had financial privacy... it ends with the college application process.*

- Your **1040 Federal Tax Return** (first two pages), a double-sided copy. If the college requires additional information, they will let you know. You can mail them that supplemental information under separate cover. The student's **1040EZ Tax Return**, one page, goes next to the parents.

- Your **Free Application for Federal Student Aid (FAFSA)** is the next item in the package. It has 103+ questions that you must answer and submit. When you receive your analysis back, it will then be called a **Student Aid Report (SAR)**, and you can print out the 103+ questions and answers page.

- A **College Expense Sheet** needs to show your own assessment of the cost of attending that specific college for nine months. The college can use this assessment to see if you did your research about the *real* cost of education, rather than just using the unrealistic catalog figure.

■ **Unusual Circumstance Paper.** This paper needs to be written each year. It should be a factual paper of your financial or employment circumstances. Your Incoming and Outgoing budget from Step One (see Financial Documents, page 39) can help here. This paper can be rewritten any time your circumstances change.

You want the college financial aid director to go back to her calculator and, using her college's formula, reduce your tuition as much as possible. With this paper she can do that. Some students receive as many as five financial aid award letters over a period of time because of new circumstantial information.

● PDFs of the **Income Tax Parent Sample, Income Tax Student Sample, Student Aid Report Sample, CSS Financial Profile, College Expense Sheet Sample, Special Unusual Circumstances Sample,** and **Parents Unusual Circumstances Sample** are available at www.JoanC Ryan.com or on the CD-ROM at the back of this book.

Statement from the Student's Family

Why does a parent, grandparents or guardian need to write a statement for the student? No one knows your teenager like you do. You know how special this unique person is and are frustrated at the thought of not being able to communicate that on the application form. Even with the myriad questions on forms, you know there are important questions that have not been asked.

Applying to college is a human being to human being experience. Do not allow an inanimate object—a form—to limit your free speech. Become familiar with using the terms *"Please see attached," "Please see enclosed,"* or *"Please see addendum."*

> *Do not allow an inanimate object—a form—to limit your free speech.*

Think about your special teenager and write up a one page paper, double-spaced or 1 1/2 spaced. Make sure the information is not redundant with what is on the form. After all, your purpose here is to submit information that was not requested but is important to know.

Why one page? Why 1 1/2 or double-spaced lines? Have mercy on your reader, please. Always keep your reader in mind. Don't scrunch the text on the page. Your readers will just not have the time to go through pages of single-spaced material. They may have bifocals, use trifocals, or have cataracts. Be kind to them.

Be succinct. Remember, *less is more.* Your job is to express, not to impress.

THE FAMILY PHOTO

I t is not just the student who is interacting with the college—it really is a family affair. It's good PR to communicate to the foundation or institution that your entire family is rooting for and working on the success of the college scholarship process. This is just one more piece of the "personal touch" that will allow the student to stand out in a crowd of applicants.

A family photo gives your readers a visual. It puts a face on your family and on your life. The members of the student's family will hopefully become active members in parents' association groups and contribute time, talent, and treasure long after their student has graduated. It is the enthusiasm, ideas, commitment, and loyalty of the parents that will infuse the Board of Trustees, that will keep faculty on their toes putting their best foot forward.

Get the family together—the whole family, grandparents too—for an informal photo. Gather all the dogs, cats, birds, and other animals that your family considers part of the family and include them in the photo along with the humans.

THE THANK-YOU SENTENCE

College is about a fifth of your real education. Your parents, grandparents, culture, siblings, fellow parishioners, neighborhood, school, friends, teammates, co-workers,

College is about a fifth of your real education.

travel, recreation, associations—all these influences give you a real-life education that adds a beautiful flavor and aroma to each and every subject in your college classes.

Always remember where you came from. Whether positive or negative, there is always a lesson learned that can be used constructively in each new adventure. Show your readers how the adults in your life model positive powers of example for you.

Accompany your photo with a brief statement, called the "thank-you sentence." This sentence is important, because it ties all your previous statements together, finishing up with gratitude and a willingness to provide even more information if the committee requests. Show honesty, cooperation, and open-mindedness in your sentence. Here's a sample.

> *Thank you for reviewing this application. Both my family and I have worked very hard to answer all of your questions completely so that you may make a confident decision regarding my request for scholarship money from your foundation. If your committee should have any further questions, I would be happy to answer them for you.*

● A PDF of the **Family Photo** is available at www.JoanCRyan.com or on the CD-ROM at the back of this book.

Follow-up Homework

So parents, after you have created and packaged up a master **College Application Package** for our student, you will have forms from each college that need to be hand-carried to your high school's guidance department. Make sure guidance has the complete list of colleges to which you are applying. Make sure the teachers, faculty, and staff that have been chosen to write confidential letters of recommendation are notified as early in September as possible.

Most high school guidance departments will be sending out their evaluation forms, confidential teacher recommendations, official transcripts, and SAT scores separately from your family-completed College Application Package.

Phone or contact guidance in person to confirm that they have sent out these forms long before the college's deadline date. When they confirm that they have, phone the Admissions department of the college, ask them to find these reports in your file, and confirm that they are, indeed, holding them in their hands.

If the college admission's staff tells you they do not have them, you need to go to guidance in person and stay there until these papers are mailed out electronically.

At the same time, it's a good idea to ask Admissions to confirm that they are holding your family-completed College Application Package. Again, treat this package as if it is worth $50,000—it may be!

Students, remember to send those handwritten thank-you notes to guidance counselors, coaches, teachers, and all who supplied you with letters. Record and date this information.

High-Tech or Low-Tech?

With all our high-tech tools, why should a person prepare a hard copy College Application Package, rather than an electronic one? Because this journey—applying for college, getting accepted to college, and attending the college—is a completely *human* experience—in the beginning, middle, and end. The nature of the beast demands hard copy. *When in Rome...*

COLLEGE INTERVIEWS

So you have mailed out your family-completed College Application Package to Admissions and have requested a personal interview. Next, you'll want to speak on the phone with the college admission's officer, who is already familiar with you from your Introduction Packet and now has your College Application Package in her hands and knows all about you. You set up a day and time for this interview.

Our student arrives for her appointment on time and, lo and behold, is told that the admission's officer is out ill and being replaced by a person of equal rank but from another department. He cannot find your application; he cannot find your package; he cannot find you on the computer. He cannot find *you*. He is frustrated, upset, impatient, stressed, and embarrassed.

Time to remember your training as an Eagle Scout. "Be Prepared" was the motto, and being prepared will serve you extremely well in this situation. It's in your best interest to always attend interviews with a complete hard copy of your College Application Package tucked into your sleek briefcase (or tasteful tote, if you'd rather). Then you can say to the *fill-in* interviewer, who knows nothing about you and doesn't know how to find anything on you, *"No worries, I have everything you need in order to conduct a thorough interview,"* and you hand him your College Application Package. When you look at his astonished face, you see a picture of relief, gratitude, and confidence.

> *When you look at his astonished face, you see a picture of relief, gratitude, and confidence.*

In a sense, you are interviewing the interviewer—not the other way around. Prepare a list of questions regarding this college, your program, procedures, employment assistance after your receive your degree, how and when the Board of Trustees meet, what are your appeal opportunities for changed policies.

Even though your SAT scores and federal financial information have been sent electronically, it is imperative that you also submit hard copies of these reports. Right next to these unofficial copies is another sheet of paper with just one important sentence on it: *"Official SAT scores have been electronically sent to you on 6.15.12."* So when the interviewer cannot find your electronic reports, he doesn't have to put your application in the "waiting for more info" pile. You have supplied him with all the necessary information he needs to function.

Even though guidance has sent their confidential letters of recommendation separately, you have copies of *open* letters of recommendation from people in all walks of life.

Your unofficial transcripts are there for the interviewer to analyze. When he puts all your information together, he can see that each paper substantiates the next piece of paper and verifies the next piece of paper. He will have trust in your unofficial transcript information. You have presented him with a "truth packet" and he knows it!

> *You have presented him with a "truth packet" and he knows it!*

THE ACCEPTANCE LETTER

I've heard, "The whole process is surreal until the acceptance letter comes in!" many times over the years. It is, indeed, true.

When you, the soon-to-be college student, receive your college acceptance letter, look to see who sent it. In most cases, it needs to be signed by the Dean of Admissions in order to be authentic. It has probably come by snail mail and is on the college letterhead. It is probably in color. Please make ten color copies of this original right away, and place the original in your safe box.

Then divide the ten copies in half. Mom files five copies of the letter inside her at-home scholarship file box inside the *Acceptance* file folder. And our student files his five copies of the letter inside his portable accordion scholarship box in the *Acceptance* file folder. (See page 100 for more on organizing.)

SPREADING THE WORD

It is important for the scholarship committee members to know that you have been accepted by college Admissions—and even more wonderful for them to know that there are multiple colleges that want you! When scholarship foundations see that other people (Admissions and college Financial Aid) are investing in you, they feel more comfortable investing in you, too. These acceptance letters are evidence—the proof—that your high school work, grades, extracurricular activities, essays, and letters of recommendation have passed muster at the college level.

Keep in mind that your *readers*, your *audience,* are actually making a business decision about what is best for their college or their scholarship foundation. These acceptance letters speak volumes and place you in their "asset" column.

Multiple acceptance letters are also beneficial when applying for *private* scholarship money. Acceptance letters inserted into the scholarship package tend to separate you from the crowd of applicants. It shows the scholarship committee volunteers that the student and parents have browsed, shopped, selected, applied, and have been accepted by multiple colleges, and in a timely manner.

Some high school seniors say they are going to college and apply for outside scholarships, but in the end, they do not go for a variety of reasons. How can the scholarship committee volunteers tell, by reading stacks and stacks of scholarship application forms, which students will actually attend?

The college acceptance letters separate you—the focused student—from the crowd of applicants. Based on these documents, the foundation believes you will be a safe investment for their funds.

● A PDF of the **Acceptance Letter Sample** is available at www.Joan CRyan.com or on the CD-rom at the back of this book.

The Really, Really Important Financial Aid Letter

When the college financial aid award letter arrives, a cover letter usually accompanies it asking whether the financial aid is accepted or rejected. *Always accept.* This does not mean you are accepting the college admissions; it means exactly what it says: *Do you accept or reject this financial aid?* You can negotiate or appeal later on, after you have received all college financial aid award letters. You can make sound comparisons with factual figures.

After you check off "accept," the very next action is to copy the letters and put the originals in a safe box, amending your "safe box inventory list" each time you add a document.

Parents, print out and fill in with pencil the "college tuition graph" as a rough draft, and customize it to your child's personal circumstances. As offers of financial aid arrive from the colleges applied to, pencil in the figures in the appropriate blocks. Have a family discussion to size up where you stand financially with your student's first-choice college.

Negotiating with the College

Before you make a call to any college, make a list of your questions, have all financial aid award letters ready to be faxed to the college, and have the **Financial Aid Comparison Graph** at hand, ready to erase and change any figures that the financial aid director modifies over the phone.

Then make the call. Communicate with the director that her college is your student's first choice, and ask if there is a way to negotiate a better deal. Would she please find a way to make this financial picture as good—or better—than what you have been offered by her competitor college? Let her know that your child would be willing to go to any lengths to cooperate with her to make this possible, even by carrying a double major or minoring in another department. This other department may be able to offer an additional grant or scholarship that would satisfy your bottom line concerns.

After all is said and done, you may receive multiple *new* financial aid award letters in the mail. Items might switch around. The colleges may now offer you less work–study and more grant money, or no work–study and more federal loan money.

When all your follow-up award letters are in, you are at the point where *the rubber meets the road.* Fill in—in ink this time—your bottom-line figures for each college and save this paper.

> *You are at the point where* the **rubber meets the road.**

WHEN ALL THE LIGHTS ARE GREEN... GO!

This is how you will know your lights are all green:
- When you find a college that has your **major**.
- When that same college **accepts** you into their fantastic program in your major.
- When that same college offers you the highest **college grant**.
- When that same college offers you the most **college scholarship** money.
- When that same college offers you the highest **inside private scholarship**.
- When that same college offers you the most **sports/art/music scholarship** money.
- When that same college offers you the highest **matching scholarship**.
- When that same college offers you the most **recruitment** money.
- When that college offers your major in a **cooperative work–study plan**.
- When that same college offers you a **freshmen class bonding trip**.
- When that same college offers you **internships or clinicals** directly connected with your major.
- When that same college guarantees you a **job** in your major when you receive your degree.

- When that same college guarantees you an **annual salary** from that job to cover all federal and college loans.

You *must* grasp that the above checklist is *what matters the most*. The list below are items all colleges have available to the student—but those are the crumbs. You don't want the crumbs. Go for the gold—the best. Concentrate on selecting the college that best matches the above items. And, depending on your Estimated Family Contribution (EFC) number, consider it a match:

- When that same college offers you the highest Supplemental Educational Opportunity Grant (SEOG).
- When that same college offers you the highest Pell Grant.
- When that same college offers you the highest Federal Stafford Loan, subsidized.
- When that same college offers you the highest Federal Stafford Loan, unsubsidized.
- When that college offers you the highest Perkins Loan.
- When that college offers you the highest college loan.
- When that college offers you the most work–study.

Line up all your college financial aid award letters and make a comparison. The college with the most checks in the top part wins! You take home the gold!

> *The college with the most checks in the top part wins!*

Keep an open mind: the college that wins may not be your first choice. But there is good reason to choose the college with the most green lights. You will find out that reason after you have attended the college for a time.

THE CHOICE IS MADE

After you have chosen your matchmaker college from the winner of your Financial Aid Comparison Graph, formally notify all the other colleges that you are withdrawing your name from their list because you have accepted another choice. Send thank-you notes to the directors of Admissions and the directors of Financial Aid at each of those colleges.

You now have a new financial partner in your life—your chosen college. When this chosen college sees that you are continually receiving outside private scholarship money, they can free up money to "purchase" another student that they are trying to woo. They love this! They now have a new financial partner in their life.

At this time, you will be converting your Financial Aid Comparison Graph from a multiple list of colleges to just the one college in which you've enrolled. Change your entries to *Freshman, Sophomore, Junior, Senior,* and *Master's* or *Post-Graduate.* You will be able to easily follow your financial track every year of college.

ENROLLED FINANCIAL AID COMPARISON WORKSHEET

You have now chosen your college and have sent out your acceptance paper to that college in certified mail—well before the usual May 1 deadline.

Now you need to create an **Enrolled College Tuition Tracking Graph**. This will be done in pencil, as your college financial aid award letters will keep shifting according to your success with your outside private scholarship awards. This worksheet will track the cost of your chosen college each year—where your money is coming from and how much money is being received. You can subtract your monies received from your college cost and figure the balance. You'll know exactly where you stand each and every year. You can enter the categories in a software program like Excel, but I would caution you about using a computer for this exercise. Get a pencil with an eraser and *own* the numbers.

You can customize your graph for your college. Some colleges give out matching funds when a student receives a certain scholarship from somewhere else. Some churches and businesses also give out matching funds, so this may be one customized category you want to place in your personal graph.

If you are going into the military, or your college has a co-op program, or your college pays you to recruit other students who get accepted, you can continue to customize your graph in every area that you will be receiving money.

In my sample, I have separated college money received,

then a balance, and then the money that does *not* come from the financial aid director of a college. You can see two sets of figures. The chart includes college money (federal, inside private, and endowment scholarships) and all other places from which you receive money. So, you may receive $25,000 total from the college financial aid director who has the power of the purse strings, but the college cost $50,000, so you know you need to get $25,000 from outside sources.

USING YOUR GRAPH TO YOUR ADVANTAGE

Find out the criteria the college uses to raise your amount. Maybe you have a GPA of 3.0—but they give out $10,000 more if you have a GPA of 3.5, and maybe $20,000 if you have a GPA of 3.7 or higher, plus strong letters of recommendation and activities and are choosing a major at their college in a department which has strong financial flexibility. It may be that their science department has ten times more money to give out than their philosophy department.

Your graph records monies based on the year you are in college—freshman, sophomore, junior, senior, Master's. You have it in your power to raise your college income by using your graph to visualize your yearly improvement.

BE PREPARED!

Be sure to print out the PDF entitled **Go with the Flow Joe** from the website. It is a chart that compares a student who uses the methods outlined in this book versus a student who "goes with the flow." The go with the flow student is way behind, not prepared and the family is totally stressed out. And at the end, many scholarships are left untouched on the table by the student who goes with the flow.

Be prepared and work the system!

● PDFs of the **Financial Aid Comparison Graph, Enrolled College Tuition Tracking Graph,** and **Go With the Flow Joe** available at www .JoanCRyan.com or on the CD-ROM at the back of this book.

STEP THREE

EDUCATIONAL AND PRIVATE SCHOLARSHIP MONEY

KEEPING THE SCHOLARSHIP MONEY FLOWING

Congratulations! You've been admitted and have some college financial aid. But the work doesn't stop there. You still need to apply for outside scholarships. And you still have three more years of undergraduate school and then that Master's degree to pay for.

UNDERSTANDING HOW SCHOLARSHIPS GET CREATED

How *do* scholarships get created? Some scholarships are written right at a kitchen table on a yellow legal pad. Someone's loved one passes away, and the family's love for him is so great—and his influence is so profound—that the family is compelled to have the beloved person's memory continue on through a scholarship.

Some scholarships are written in the board room of a law firm. That might be a client of the law firm who wants the interest on a trust fund to be given away as an educational scholarship.

Another scholarship may be written in the back of a barber shop. If the barber discovers that creating a private scholarship is a tax deduction, he is delighted to set up the offering.

A scholarship may be written in the back of a barber shop.

Some people just bring their check to the local high school authorities and say, "please give this to some kid who wants to become a nurse." Look up your state's Attorney General, Division of Charitable Trusts web page. Many of the scholarships or grants are for 501c3 non-profit corporations, but mixed in are also some monies for individuals and education.

Any company, corporation, or institution can give away money any way it chooses. Some of these companies do not want the work of administering these scholarships, so they send the criteria to the local high school or town hall. Scholarship committee volunteers meet at the high school cafeteria to work on all the applications sent in and choose the students who will receive each different scholarship.

So, no matter where they originate, our goal is to find them, apply for them, and track them diligently. How do you keep track of all the myriad pieces of paper that you and others generate in the scholarship process? Staying organized is critical for this entire process. And here is how you do it!

MAKING CHANGES TO YOUR SYSTEM

Remember that sorter bin for college applications you created in Step Two? Now it's time to convert the sorter bin from a *college application* system to a *scholarship application* system.

Because this process is date-sensitive and cyclical, the names and order of your labels will be different, and the scholarship application package will be thinner.

Create at least three "mini-packets," comprised of the Personal Profile Paper, your core essay, and resume. Always have a packet ready to hand out when you need one. Keep one on the passenger side of the car, the kitchen counter, or in your backpack.

For the benefit of expediency (and saving trees), it is perfectly okay in this private arena to double-side copies of your information. The exception is the essays—no back-to-back essays, please. Definitely double-side your CSS Financial Profile, reducing six sheets of paper down to three. Your income tax forms can also be double-sided. Recommendation letters that are over one page may be double-sided. Most of the remaining enclosures should be single-sided.

What is the difference of order? Examine the PDF of the **Sorter Bin Label Comparison** and the **Scholarship Application Package List.** You'll see that your individual SAT reports are no longer necessary; they will have all been recorded in your high school transcript. (But check on this. If your high school has decided to stop this practice, double-side copy the SAT report onto the back of your transcript.)

Schedule days and times that you will work solely on applying to private scholarships—both inside and outside. This will soon become your new part-time job.

NOW YOU HAVE A WHOLE DIFFERENT AUDIENCE

When you were writing and producing papers for your College Application Package, your audience was made of academia: teachers, guidance counselors, college admission directors, college financial aid directors, recruiters, and interviewers. All the people who read your College Application Package had one thing in common. They were academics—educators who have a laser-like focus on what they were looking for in your information. They were looking at numbers and restricted recommendations. They were looking at vacancies in their programs. They were thinking, "After we choose the crème de la crème, we need 63 artists, one football player, 11 math mongers, one piano player, and three language students."

Now you are in a totally different arena. Inside private college scholarships and outside private scholarships come from anyone and everyone, formally educated or not. They have a much wider criteria in what they are looking for. They also use *all* of their background experience to judge your package, not just what they learned in school.

For example, someone's great-grandmother, who has since passed away, could have set up a $500 inside private college scholarship for any female from Boston who is enrolled in the Nursing Program at Tufts and is specializing in Geriatrics. Note that this is a "private inside college scholarship." It is *not* a college scholarship, per se. The money is not coming out of the pockets of the college. The money is coming out of the interest on the principal of the great-grandmother's trust.

Your audience, therefore, becomes her family, who are trustees of that account. You will be creating and mailing your Scholarship Application Package to their home. The family knew their great-grandmother and her mission, and they know she would go for the underdog every time. She would choose a student not with the highest numbers, but the student that could show grit and overcome difficult obstacles; a student who was able, through her core essay, to persuade her audience of her love of nursing.

Most private scholarship audiences want to know all about *you*. They are not interested just in numbers. They are interested in you as an individual. They wonder, "Are you a risk-free investment? If we give you our grandmother's money, are you the type of young person who will not even finish your freshman year at college and leave? Or are you the type of student who loves what you are doing so much that you will excel and flourish?"

For these applications, unrestricted letters of recommendation are very important. Letters from neighbors, peers, relatives, parish priest, doctor, dentist, scout master, barber, or volunteer supervisors about their personal experience with you and your character count a lot. If you were once compared to "Dennis, the Menace" but have turned a corner in your life, surely one of the above people will have observed it and will write about it.

Who Is Your Scholarship Application Package Audience?

Who might be making the final judgment as to whether you deserve to get the nod? This is just a sampling of who these readers might be:

Teachers, plumbers, bankers, farmers, singers, real estate agents, priests, ministers, rabbis, travel agents, city councilmen and -women, stockbrokers, electricians, artists, computer techs, retired folks, supermarket managers, waitresses, small business men and women, carpenters, mothers and fathers, insurance agents, military veterans, nurses, grandparents, airline pilots, radio broadcasters, ski instructors, accountants.

And these folks are Catholics, Protestants, Jews, Muslims, atheists, agnostics, republicans, democrats, independents, libertarians, socialists, and communists. They all have one thing in common—they are *volunteers*.

SCHOLARSHIPS ARE EVERYWHERE!

There are scholarships for everything that you already naturally do in your life.

Grocery Shopping: Parents, when you do your weekly food shopping, bring a notepad. As you are working through your shopping list and picking up items, such as Heinz Ketchup, read the label on the bottle, and look for information about contests or scholarship money being offered.

Clothes Shopping: When you are shopping for clothing, itemize each piece of clothing by writing down the name on the label and article of clothing. Don't forget shoes, boots, and slippers. When you get home, look up that company on the Internet to see if they are offering contests, scholarships, or educational opportunities. Phone customer service managers and speak directly with them.

Sports Shopping: Every article of clothing, equipment, and accessories—your hockey uniform, ice skates, socks, hockey stick, puck, and gloves—has a label. Look up the company for contests, scholarships, and educational opportunities.

Car Shopping: Look up everything about your new car—the tires, the radio, the CD player. Jot down all those companies' names and research them for opportunities.

Vacations: Check your airline, train, or bus company for opportunities. Research your luggage and camera companies. Ask the manager of the ski club if they offer any opportunities for members.

Insurance Companies: Check your home, life, health, and automobile insurance companies for opportunities.

Furniture Shopping: Do the drill. Don't forget the lamps and carpet companies.

Home Shopping: All your office supply and equipment companies. Dishes, glasses, pots and pans—leave nothing out.

● PDFs of the **Sorter Bin Label Comparison** and **Scholarship Application Package List** are available at www.JoanCRyan.com or on the CD-ROM at the back of this book.

THE GOOD, THE BAD, AND THE UGLY

Typical of the rest of life, it's not always rosy. Behind every lovely facet of life is a dark cloud. This is also true for scholarships. Ignorance is not bliss, so here is a bit of a reality check around the topic of scholarships.

GOOD NEWS

The good news is that generous people, companies, and institutions give of their time, talent, and money to total strangers for the purpose of education.

BAD NEWS

Bad News Number One is that scholarship foundations, whether profit and non-profit, move around like fleas on a dog. You cannot trust an address provided. Keeping up with their geographical changes is now easier with the Internet, but bear in mind that the foundation

Scholarship foundations... move around like fleas on a dog.

that used to be on First Avenue may be on Main Street this year and will be on Jones Drive next year.

When you send out the envelope with your Standard Request Letter for the application always place the words "Address Correction Requested" under your return address. If the company filled out their *change of address* paperwork at the post office, your letter should be forwarded there. If the company has not filled out the USPS form, you will receive your letter back in the mail with the new address stamped or written on it from the post office. You will have to make another envelope with the new address on it.

When you receive the application form, always check the envelope to see if it has a new address on it. Sometimes the foundation will choose to save printing costs by printing new envelopes but keeping old letterhead. Some of the information on that letterhead could be out of date, including the Board of Trustees.

Bad News Number Two

You cannot trust the eligibility description. They may list the eligibility requirements to be a high school senior with a 3.0 GPA enrolling in a four-year college, majoring in health and human sciences. It turns out that those requirements were for last year—the Board of Trustees met *this* year and changed the requirements to a high school senior with a 3.5 GPA enrolling in a four-year college, majoring in physical therapy for males only. Just like addresses, eligibility criteria can change on an annual basis, and the only way to know for certain is to hold the *current* application in your hands.

Additionally, you cannot trust the amount of money offered or if it will be renewable each year. If the scholarship was funded by a family, and some of the family members are now out of work, most likely they will not be able to keep donating the same amount to the scholarship as when they were working. The $1,500 scholarship they were offering last year might be reduced to $800 and will not be renewable.

If the stock market and economy are in a recession, the law firm that is administering funds for their deceased client may need to make adjustments because the client's principal is down. The interest on the principal, which was going toward providing scholarship money, would also be lower.

Foundations that gave out scholarship money for students year after year to receive a Bachelor's degree and then continued to give them out toward a Master's degree, this year have eliminated scholarship offerings for the Master's degree.

Each year individuals, groups, companies, and institutions have to be realistic about what they are able to give away in the form of a scholarship. It is our job to be aware of the possibility of change and keep up with the current information from each person and group.

THE UGLY NEWS

It was my personal experience that some people are very negative about scholarships. When I would say to them "I'm going to apply for the ABC scholarship," they would respond with such negative comments. "We applied for that scholarship a couple of years back and never got a thing! It's a rip-off. What a scam! I'm never going to bother applying for a scholarship again!" They hold on to that anger and resentment for years.

When I received the scholarship application from ABC foundation, their requirements were that the student had to have been a member of a music association for at least two years, with proof of active participation, and that the music teacher had to be a member of the National Music Teachers Association. But this family was sending their child for music lessons to a neighbor who had no credentials whatsoever. The family found out later that they have been paying for music lessons from an unqualified person. They are angry at the music teacher and at themselves. They are angry that they did not have the eligibility requirements for this scholarship. They felt guilty for making a wrong choice, but instead of taking personal responsibility for that choice, they decided to point the finger of blame at the scholarship foundation.

Another family discovered an art scholarship. They brought the application to the student's art teacher only to be told, "Oh don't bother applying for this. I have never heard of anyone who has received this scholarship." Upon further investigation the family found out that this foundation has been sponsoring art scholarships for 50 years and is well respected and modeled after other art foundations. They also find out that the foundation has a policy that, for those students who applied but did not receive their scholarship, they will forward the student's application to another art scholarship foundation. The lessons learned by the student who applied to this foundation will remain with her for the rest of her life.

> *They will forward the student's application to another art scholarship foundation.*

We need to be grateful that small business owners and private families even bother to offer scholarship money. We should be shouting from the rooftops, *"Thank you."* Small business owners' scholarships keep our students in their chairs year after year. They are amazing positive examples.

> *We should be shouting from the rooftops, "Thank you."*

They work long hours, often over eight hours a day, to build their small businesses. They support their families, their churches, their communities, and somehow, in spite of all they do, they still have a passion to give away their hard-earned money to total strangers for the purpose of education. And they do this year after year. And they attempt to convince other organizations in their community to do the same. We owe them a tremendous debt of gratitude. They are the life changers.

THE ISSUE OF RESENTMENT

The high school award ceremony was held in the gym. The room was packed with hundreds of parents and students. My daughter and I had worked tirelessly for a whole year applying for private scholarships. As a result of all that hard work and the generosity of many people, my daughter was called up on stage fifteen times to accept private scholarship awards. I was so happy for her, so grateful to God for this special moment in our lives, and so grateful for this incredible memory that we would have forever fixed in our minds and hearts. But the woman sitting next to me was bristling with anger.

During the break she felt compelled to announce to anyone around her that "the girl that got so many scholarships... Well, her family *knew* people, and that's how she got them... They *knew* people. In order to get scholarships you have to know people." I responded that the student's family didn't know anyone special. That family belongs to a distinct group called *survivors. Other people want what the survivors have, but they are not willing to do what the survivors had to do to get it.*

She had no idea that I was the student's mother. I was so naive, I could not imagine someone being angry at someone else's success. I was an orphan and a single-parent mom, financially supporting my family on a little hospital paycheck. I had lived through breast cancer, spine injury, and meningitis—and there was my daughter who had to put her supermarket paycheck toward paying our heat and utility bills. I was really taken aback by this woman's behavior. *I* certainly did not know *people.*

Even in the most wonderful cause, there are some people who will not be happy for you.

What I did know is that I would never change the opinion or character of such a person, and I did not feel the need to try. And what I *do* know is that she taught me an important lesson. *Even in the most wonderful cause, there are some people who will not be happy for you.*

Let them own their *own* issues. Do what is right for your family and your student, and let the rest roll off.

That night became known as the *Catherine Schwartz Night* at Winnacunnet High School Awards Ceremony.

Some Sage Advice about Scholarships

Where Do I Apply for Money?

There are innumerable places to harvest money to help you pay for school. As in a garden, you have to do the digging, hoeing, and cultivating, but hard work pays off. So let's get going! Here are ten places to get you started.

1. **The Federal Government:** Pell, Stafford, SEOG, and Perkins. In November, go online or to your Guidance Department or Financial Aid Office and obtain your FAFSA; fill out, sign, print, copy, and submit your FAFSA as close to January 2 as possible—but not before! Don't wait for your W-2. Estimate your taxes!

2. **The State Government:** Make sure you applied for *all* state government grants. For example, there is the New Hampshire Incentive Grant and The New Hampshire Charitable Fund, just to name a couple.

3. **The City or Town Government:** Request scholarship applications for *resident* student aid. Go to your local high school guidance office for *local* student aid.

4, **The College:** Your college should offer you some *grant* monies. Check your Financial Aid Award letter. Ask the financial aid director how his college handles outside private scholarship money. You want to make sure that they decrease *loans*—and not *grants*.

5. **Inside Private Scholarships:** These are scholarships donated by the private sector for students attending that college only. Ask the college's financial aid office for this list. Inquire specifically about *athletic* money.

6. **Outside Private Scholarships and Grants:** These are the foundations that are *national*, *regional*, and *local.* Apply

even if you believe you are only remotely eligible. Second-guessing the committee members' decision is a big mistake.

7. **Work–Study Program:** Federal jobs around campus are usually minimum wage, and the check is made out directly to the student—not the college. This can be excellent personal spending money!

8. **Dependents or Spouses of Employees:** Check with parents' corporations for information about scholarships or educational benefits for *children of employees.* If you are married, check your spouse's corporation for scholarship and educational benefits.

9. **Residency Advisor:** This is usually offered after the student's freshman year, but a word of caution: *do this only as a last resort.* RAs are like college dorm babysitters. When someone in the dorm needs assistance with a broken bureau, more heat, less heat, or a new bed, it's the RA who makes the necessary phone calls to fix the problem. On the other hand, some colleges give you free room and board with this job.

10. **Family Associations, Community Newspapers, Local Banks, etc.:** Italian-American Club, American Legion, sports associations, churches, unions, magazine subscriptions—the list goes on.

DON'T SHY AWAY FROM APPLYING

Even if you think you are just remotely eligible, go ahead and apply. You cannot know who else is applying for a scholarship. Making *assumptions* is the enemy of being a successful scholarship recipient. Of all the applications that the scholarship committee pours over, it may turn out that your application package most closely resembles their perfect candidate.

For example, a scholarship committee had received 30 applications by the deadline date. They were pouring over these applications and were disappointed with most of what they had received. There was one applicant who had only a couple of their eligibility requirements, but they were impressed with her "package." During the discussion, one of the scholarship committee members noted some information on the student's Personal Profile Paper. The student wrote "Fed and watered ten Belgian, *gentle giant* horses every morning at 4:00 AM for four years during high school."

This committee member stood up and began to speak passionately about what this short statement represented—reliability and dependability in a long-term relationship. In his opinion, this student should receive the scholarship. As it turns out, he was a farmer and knew full well the mental, physical, spiritual, and emotional commitment that this required. In his expertise, showing up and performing this task daily, year after year, spoke volumes about the student.

That student was selected for the scholarship because she had the willingness to do the work and create the package for an organization, and submit it *knowing full well* that she had only a couple of their requirements. She understood that if her application ended up on their table, they would at least read it. She was willing to be rejected, but was not. This one powerful statement was enough to bring her over the top.

By power of example, the entire Scholarship Application Package shows your seriousness of purpose, your determination, your attention to detail, your respect for your readers, your ability to organize, your ability to meet deadlines, and your ability to follow directions. You need only to receive three or four good private scholarship awards to make a significant difference in your total financial aid package. But in order to get those three or four, many applications are required.

THE SPIRIT AND LETTER OF THE LAW

The difference between *The Spirit of the Law* and *The Letter of the Law* in Scholarship Land is the unspoken subtlety of the process. What does that mean? It refers to *soft* language versus *hard* language. When the student is filling out a scholarship application, it behooves them to read instructions carefully. Some scholarship foundations will write something like this:

Fill out this application, attach your essay and make sure we receive it no later than December 1.

This instruction is what I call the *Spirit of the Law*—the language is *soft*. It is very flexible, very open, certainly inviting. I would send this foundation a "complete scholarship application package"—approximately 20 pages.

Now, another foundation may write up their instructions like this:

Fill out and send only our application form. All other attachments will immediately disqualify you. Our deadline date is December 1. Applications received after that date will be discarded.

This is what I call the *Letter of the Law*—the language is *hard*. There's no wiggle room here. Do exactly as they ask.

MATCHING SCHOLARSHIPS

Opportunities abound in so many places. Stay sharp and pay attention to everything. There may be some money waiting for you—you just have to be aware it exists. For instance, anyone or any institution, foundation, or company can create a matching scholarship—it could be your own church. It could be set up like this:

The Smithtown Methodist Church is offering a $500 matching scholarship to any student who is a member of our parish, is currently active in our parish, and has been accepted into Boston University who also offers this student a scholarship. We will match it up to $500. The scholarship information can be found in the Business Office of the college.

The bottom line: 1) you have to be a member of the church, 2) you have to be currently active in the parish, 3) you have to be accepted by a particular college, and 4) that college has to have offered you a scholarship.

● A PDF of the **Abraham Burtman Charity Sample** is available at www .JoanCRyan.com or on the CD-ROM at the back of this book.

TIPS FOR SUCCESS IN APPLYING FOR SCHOOL MONEY

1. Use your at-home file box and portable accordion box (see Step One, Tools of the Trade).

   • Alphabetize all the documents to be inserted into your package.

   • The 12 month *Deadline Date* folders are for the actual, current, physical application forms.

   • Enrolled college file folders are for the college departments and offices with which you are dealing, such as Admissions, Financial Aid, or Study Abroad.

2. Shop through your list of foundations for those that you need to apply to and check them off. Send a request for an application via an email address, if possible. If not, use snail mail.

3. Address envelopes with "ADDRESS CORRECTION REQUESTED" directly under your return address.

4. Create an FAQ (Frequently Asked Questions) sheet. Copy this and keep it handy in a sheet protector next to your computer. You will refer to it often.

5. When you receive your *current* scholarship application, read the deadline date and place this application in the appropriate *Deadline Date* monthly folder.

6. Two months before deadline date, begin typing applications. Read the foundation's philosophy carefully. Tweak your core essay to address their interests. Be aware of *hard* language versus *soft* language in their instructions (see The Spirit and Letter of the Law, page 155). Ninety-five percent of your applications will be packaged according to the **Private Scholarship Record Keeping Chart**. Submit everything about yourself even if you are not asked to do so.

7. After you have typed up the application with all the necessary attachments, copy the blank Private Scholarship Record Keeping Chart and fill in the information to show the actions you have taken with each foundation. Remember, it can take up to seven days for mail to reach West Coast foundations.

8. When you receive an award, finish filling out your Private Scholarship Record Keeping Chart. Make sure you send a handwritten thank-you note, along with confirmation of the name of your college, its address, its financial aid director's name, your college ID number, and any other information the foundation may require, such as the tuition bill.

When you are invited to a foundation's award ceremony, make sure you drop everything else and show up.

9. When you are invited to a foundation's award ceremony, make sure you drop everything else and show up.

10. During each school break, send a note and photos to the foundations that have given you an award. Fill them in on how and what you are doing, learning, enjoying, or struggling with, and the opportunities you have experienced through their generosity.

11. Make yourself a short customized checklist of what you need to do to request and apply for each package in this order:

   a. Create a list of names and addresses of scholarships
   b. Request the application form
   c. Make a copy of the original
   d. Type a rough draft on the copy
   e. Bring it to your parents to proof and tweak
   f. Type finished original application
   g. Copy finished original application
   h. Have parent collate and create your package
   i. Record all action taken on checklist

j. Type address labels for 10 x 13 envelopes

k. Place package in envelope. Secure and mail

Having a Good Family System

To navigate the maze of applying for school money, most families create the system that works best for them.

For example, as a high school senior, the student's job may be to get the names and addresses of as many scholarship foundations as possible and to enter that information in Excel. The student sends out the Standard Request Letters and, when the applications arrive, the student does the typing of the applications.

The parents' job is to proof and tweak any errors on both the rough draft and final version.

Together they collate, create, record, and mail each package. It is important that each partner is familiar with these job descriptions because once the student goes to college, the jobs change. Both teammates need to have a working knowledge of the whole process.

When the student attends college, the parent does all of the scholarship application processing. The student's responsibility is to make sure he receives at a minimum a GPA of 3.0. He will also be responsible for sending his parent all important college documents and correspondence in a timely manner. Both parties need to set aside a time of day once a week to have a phone discussion about coordinating scholarship information. Both parent and student must have their at-home file box and at-school portable box filled with the same current papers.

When the student comes home on break, the family needs to set aside a time to go over both boxes to match the contents and ensure accuracy.

Private Scholarship
Record Keeping Chart

A **Private Scholarship Record Keeping Chart** needs to be filled out as you go along in compiling your package. This chart is for the parents' use—it is not sent out to anyone.

Make a dozen or so blank copies of this form to have on hand as you collate each of your scholarship application packages. You keep this in your *Scholarships Applied For* folder. Attach it to your personal copy of the application. It will help you keep track of the who, what, where, when, and how of each package. Take your time filling it out before you place it into the package. Do not assume you can do this chart later or hurriedly fill it out at supper time. This is how mistakes are made.

> *Do not assume you can do this chart later or hurriedly fill it out at supper time.*

If you need to communicate important information to yourself for a future reference and there is no space, make a note on the bottom of the form, "*See more info on reverse side*," and then carefully write the additional information on the back of the page. Remember, you will need to be able to read your own handwriting. Abbreviations that you used in November may not make sense to you in March.

Most of your packages will contain the "regular" list of contents. However, there will be those foundations that require something a little different—or more or less information. It's highly unlikely that you will remember the contents of a package you sent to "Foundation A" way back in November. But you *do* need to know. The Private Scholarship Record Keeping Chart will tell you.

All sorts of circumstances may come up. After weeks of

reading and considering your application, the foundation's scholarship committee might misplace your package and need a new one. Some member took it on vacation with them to read and lost it. Maybe the U.S. Postal Service lost it. A dog ate it. You need to resend them the *exact* same package as the first time. No problem! You're prepared.

> *A dog ate it. You need to resend them the* exact *same package as the first time.*

When you receive a scholarship award letter from "Foundation A," you remove your record keeping chart from the *Scholarships Applied For* folder and place it into the *Scholarships Received* folder along with any correspondence from this foundation.

Now handwrite your thank-you note, record that on your chart, and see that you revisit this chart in December, before you go home for Christmas vacation. Why? Because in December you want to send a progress note and photos (see #10, page 158). Then you will go to your *Scholarships Received* folder and record that you have sent the progress reports.

You will be filling out new Private Scholarship Package Record Keeping Charts every year.

● A PDF of the **Private Scholarship Record Keeping Chart** is available at www.JoanCRyan.com or on the CD-ROM at the back of this book.

KEEP THOSE CARDS AND LETTERS COMING

Dancing about the living room is quite appropriate, once the acceptance letters begin rolling in! Take time to celebrate the results of your hard work.

THE ACCEPTANCE LETTERS

The wonderful effect of applying Early Decision, Early Action, or Rolling is that you receive most of your acceptance letters before Christmas. This is important because you need these letters for your *outside scholarship* application packets. Most scholarship applications have definite deadline dates. That date can be as early as November or December of your high school senior year, so you want to get these acceptance letters into your scholarship packets as early as possible.

I know... some of your friends have not even applied to college yet. They are thinking April and May. Please, do not compare yourself with other families. The money, the peace, the time, and the joy all come from being ahead of the game. Why wait to scramble for bread crumbs?

You are the customer. The college is the company. The product is education. Go to the sale early. Get your full value while the limited supply lasts.

As we discussed in Step Two, when you receive your college acceptance letters, place the color copies into your scholarship packages with early deadline dates.

Place these college acceptance letters right after your scholarship application form in your packet. Right up front. The acceptance letters speak volumes to your readers. These letters separate you from the crowd, big time.

Once you have determined the college you'll be attending, you'll need to include just a single acceptance letter. But you cannot choose your college until you receive your financial aid award letters from all the colleges you have applied to—until the "back and forth" negotiations are completed. When your family has completely finished this process, then you will be accepting one college for admittance and one college for money. Only after all this action has taken place do you omit the runner-up college contenders from your package.

THE TRUST BEGINS

These college acceptance letters are important to the scholarship committee members in deciding who they will choose. These members are making a business decision. Which applicant has the lowest risk—the

> *The acceptance letters prove that you have been "vetted."*

guaranteed investment? When they see that you have been accepted by college faculty, it will prompt them to look twice at your scholarship application. The acceptance letters prove that you have been "vetted." The mere fact that you have made applications to colleges early, have been accepted early, and are now applying for scholarship money shows that you are serious about college.

The scholarship committee members know full well that not everyone who receives their money will actually finish college. But they are looking for the dependable, reliable, and persistent applicants. They want to ensure that their money gets used for its intended goal—a college degree. The acceptance letters place a nail into the coffin of doubt.

MAKING THE CHOICE

Okay, the college acceptance letters have come in, and because you applied to all institutions early, they came in *before* Christmas. Now it is decision time for you, so you need to go back to the When All Lights Are Green... Go section (see page 137) and follow the instructions with faith. After you've chosen your college, your package will contain just one college acceptance letter, as we discussed above.

CORRESPONDENCE WITH THE CHOSEN COLLEGE

You will be receiving lots of correspondence from your chosen college—papers to fill out and sign. If you have been awarded a work–study job, see if you will be able to select working in Admissions, the Financial Aid Department, or the Business Office. *These are departments where brand-new scholarship information can be obtained and you would be on the front lines of knowing about them.*

In your college correspondence, you will also be assured of a place in your chosen program. You need to sign off on your program and choose electives. Choosing electives can be like standing before a smorgasbord... *I'll take one of these and three of those.* But, please, in your first year, you need to be extremely conservative in making time choices. There will be ample opportunities throughout college to explore more. First get a solid foundation.

> *Choosing electives can be like standing before a smorgasbord.*

Once you have chosen your freshman class schedule and it has been accepted, you need to ask the college for your *official undergraduate enrollment verification course selection form.* This paper proves to the scholarship committee members that not only are you accepted, but that you are officially in that college's program. Now you have two "big guns" papers that absolutely separate you from the field of scholarship foundation applicants.

A CHANGE TO THE SCHOLARSHIP PACKAGE

You have made a decision; you have accepted one college over all the others; you have notified all the other colleges of your decision. Now, the *order* of your scholarship package changes.

Copy the acceptance letter—in color—from your chosen college. On the back, copy the official undergraduate enrollment verification course selection form. (If your college does not use a form with this name, use your first semester course schedule or a copy of the deposit on your dorm room.) This new double-sided color copy goes into your "acceptance letter" section.

Now that you are an official member of this college and your specific program, ask Admissions if there are any special freshman programs that take place *before* school starts. For example, there may be a LaVida five-day hiking trip in August *for freshmen only*.

Please take advantage of this wonderful offer. To be able to bond with your new freshman class before you meet them in daily classes will take away pounds of stress and pressure. You will already know some of your classmates inside and out. You will already have a close-knit support group!

Congratulations!

THE ANTICIPATED FUNDS PAPER

The **Anticipated Funds** paper is our new kid on the block. This is one of the most useful papers you will write for Scholarship Application Package purposes. Most of the scholarship foundations will ask you again and again to supply this information. Even for those who do not ask, it's a good idea to supply this important financial picture.

This paper is going to save you a great deal of time and energy and be helpful to the scholarship reader as well. On the application form, you can write in the anticipated funds space, "*Please see attached.*" That's it. No trying to squeeze important information into a space where it will not fit legibly; no looking in the attic or under the bed for financial information; no going through reams of files to find one answer for one question one time and then another answer for a different question another time. All your information is provided to your reader on one succinct page in every packet for every foundation.

DEALING WITH GUESSWORK

You will be asked what federal monies you will be receiving: how much and from where. The answers you give are *anticipated* answers. They are *estimates* or *approximates*, because you do not know yet. You have no control over the figures. For instance, Congress can mandate a law that says each student will receive $10,000 a year. But if that law is not *funded*, the law is barren, worthless, not worth the paper it is written on. Always look at the funding—they passed a law *and* put up the money. Trust, but verify.

So, you do the best you can to be as accurate as possible, knowing full well that Congress—or the college Board of Trustees or the college financial aid director—holds the power of the purse strings, and all of this is subject to change without notice.

As you will see in the following pages, in the Anticipated Funds paper, the word *"pending"* is important in communicating to your private scholarship reader and also to yourself.

The student's savings account balance is not pending. The parents' contribution is not pending. You have definite stats and control over your personal financial information... No *pending* here.

The figure you use in your "pending" answer needs to always be consistent *until* you have the money in your pocket. If the college says they are going *(GOING)* to give you $10,000, that doesn't mean you have it. Your financial aid award letter can change many times through a variety of circumstances. Keep using the answer *pending* until you receive the actual amount in your college account each semester.

You will be asked again and again how much cash you have; how much money is in your checking and savings account. When I finish paying my monthly bills, I know how much is left in my checking account... a minimal number to be sure. You will know, too, because you have completed your homework—the Incoming and Outgoing paper.

When the student gets a full-time summer job, and his goal is to put away for college 75 percent of his eight weeks of pay, he knows exactly what his financial goal looks like. But if a student has more than, say, $5,000 in his college savings account, he will be happily penalized by the college. He should keep that balance low by giving his parents his savings money—they will not be penalized anywhere near what he will be.

You will be asked if any family members or friends will be donating money to your college costs. Hopefully,

> *If a student has more than, say, $5,000 in his college savings account, he will be happily penalized by the college.*

you bought this book while your children were young and explained to any grandparents who wanted to put money in the student's name and social security number that it was not in the best interest of their desired outcome.

Parents know their budget numbers and need to set aside a minimum of 5 percent of the total college cost for their aid contribution. Aid from the college is a question mark and pending until first semester is over. Then you will have real incoming and outgoing figures.

Money from outside private scholarship foundations can come into your account first semester or at the end of second semester. Your answer is a question mark and pending. Nothing is in your pocket yet.

COLLEGE EXPENSE SHEET

Okay, student, now that you are fully enrolled in your chosen college, it's time to update your College Expense Sheet. You have access to the breakdown of costs for tuition, room, board, meals, lab fees, association fees, sport, music, art fees, medical insurance, and any miscellaneous fees that a college can think up. You now know the cost breakdown of your particular program, i.e. travel, sports equipment, a particular type of musical instrument, or art supplies.

Customize your new Expense Sheet, but retain all the personal charges that you had originally included, such as laundry, dental, movies, and pizza.

Some scholarship foundation committee members do not realize the costs involved in applying for their money, so let's help them out by creating a **Scholarship Expense Sheet** right along with your College Expense Sheet. This will be a checklist that you use with each application you submit. On one side of the paper you will have the College Expense Sheet information from your enrolled college and on the other side you will have Scholarship Expense Sheet breakdown. You'll need printer cartridges, printer paper, envelopes, and stamps; travel funds for personal scholarship interviews; money to buy the suit to wear for the interview. And you need tons of thank-you notecards.

● PDFs of the **Anticipated Funds Sample** and **Scholarship Expense Sheet Sample** are available at www.JoanCRyan.com or on the CD-ROM at the back of this book.

SOLIDIFYING THE PARTNERSHIP

As the scholarship-seeking process progresses, you'll find great value in partnering with the colleges. But *how* do you work as a partner with colleges?

The financial aid director usually sends a *financial aid award letter.* This letter has a detailed breakdown of the director's sources for your college money. When you receive outside private scholarship money and the checks get deposited into your college account, the director can remove loans and work–study from your award package.

By virtue of this money going into your account, you are freeing up the college's money to use for other students. By winning scholarships, you are allowing the college to "hire" additional students. It provides the director an opportunity to offer more money to another desirable student who may be considering a competing college. This puts you in a favorable light with the school.

Why is this important? The obvious fact is that it is a very positive experience to be a business partner with the school. The financial aid director looks forward each year to our student getting more outside scholarships, so then she can negotiate for more students.

But there is more to this than meets the eye. This practice of *setting yourself apart from the crowd*—this action, so successful, becomes a template for other areas of your life. In your classroom, you practice going above and beyond what is asked of you. You do the same in your family life, in your personal relationships, and in your work life. You now live out a higher standard according to your core values. You have a positive reputation in a brand-new arena.

THE TRUST BEGINS AGAIN

This time, you're building trust not with a foundation, but with an institution. At some point in the college journey, this trust will pay off. For example, imagine that one year, it just happens to work out that all of your outside private scholarships are going to be mailed to you in your second semester. They are all going to be mailed after December 15! *Where is your money to pay for the first semester?*

Because you have a track record of *trust* in acquiring multiple *outside* private scholarships, the director moves your *inside* college scholarships, your *inside* college grants, and your *inside* private scholarships—all that would have been given to you in the second semester—to the first semester. You're all set. Your college is working *with* you. Now they're *your* working partner.

Students, each year you show college faculty and administrators that you are reliable, dependable, trustworthy, self-confident, ambitious, hard-working, and accountable. They will green flag you for post-graduate alumni assistance in the future.

> *They will green flag you for post-graduate alumni assistance in the future.*

WHO ARE THESE PEOPLE ANYWAY?

A visit to your mailbox reveals envelopes with strange names piled high. In your previous life, you would probably throw these out, but now you need to open every single envelope. Any one of them could contain your scholarship award letter and check. A family foundation scholarship could have a name of The Harriet B. Smith Memorial Scholarship, but the nephew who is administering the scholarship funds has a plumbing business. He sends out your award and check in an envelope with a return address of *Joe's Plumbing*. Double-check all your mail, even if it looks like a third-class advertisement.

If you are anything like our family, you all go to the mail box together, open up the mail in the middle of the street, and find a scholarship award in the midst of all the envelopes. And then, everyone dances a jig!

TAKING CARE OF THE BUSINESS

Okay, when you are finished jumping up and down, hugging and crying with glee, here is what you do.

1. Send a handwritten thank-you note to the person who signed the letter.

2. Copy the award letter.

3. Copy both sides of the foundation's check.

4. Go to your *Scholarships Applied To* folder. Pull out and update the Record Keeping Chart. Then attach both award letter and the copy of the check to the copy of the application form for this foundation and move this whole file into the *Scholarships Received* folder.

5. Now let's take a look at the check itself. Read all the words on the check. Is it made out in your name? (Sometimes mistakes are made.) Does it have to be cashed within 30 days or 90 days? Is there any information on the face of the check that makes you want to take immediate action?

6. Open two checking accounts. Open one personal checking account for clothes, pizza, etc. Open a second one for college expenses—for tuition, room, board, and books. It is into this account that all scholarship checks should be deposited. Wait to pay your college bill until the final bill is received, because the amount tends to keep changing.

7. If a check is made out to you and the specific name of the college, hand-carry the check to the bursar at your enrolled college, sign your name *in front of the bursar,* and be sure to ask for a receipt. Now we invoke Law Number 1 again—copy everything! Please ask him to make two copies of the receipt for you. Now you have three receipts. One is your original, and two are working copies. Here's where they go:

   a. Original receipt is deposited in a safe box vault.
   b. Copy for private foundation's record keeping file.
   c. Copy for your *college bills and receipts* folder.

8. In your scholarship box on the right hand side, make a folder titled, *college bills and receipts*. Place one of your working copy receipts into this folder.

9. From your *Scholarships Received* folder, pull out the file on the foundation that wrote the check and attach the other receipt copy.

10. Request the day and time that your high school will be having its award ceremony for high school seniors and find out the deadline date for the printing of the booklets for this event.

11. Create a list of all the people, foundations, institutions, and organizations that have awarded you a scholarship and present it to the appropriate high school department well before the deadline date required by the booklet printing company.

12. Even though you may have received a scholarship check *before* your high school's award ceremony, it is nice to have the recognition of this gift at the award ceremony. Send a note to all private foundations that are awarding you scholarships, even the ones who have already sent you a check, and ask if they might come and present you with their award on such and such a day and time. This is the culmination of all your hard work. This is the time to be honored. This is the well-deserved memory.

> *This is the time to be honored. This is the well-deserved memory.*

Some of the private foundations may be putting on their own award night and may invite you to attend. You will be given ample time to give your employer notice that you need that night off. Make certain that you accept this invitation and that you *show up* to the ceremony. Have photos taken. Use a firm handshake, eye contact, and a smile! When you arrive home, handwrite your thank-you note.

MAINTAINING A BALANCE

When you receive correspondence award letters in the mail, most of them will provide important information. For example, they will say that the award is for $1,200 and then they will tell you how it is to be paid out to you: $600 for first semester and $600 for second semester. Record this information in your *Scholarships Received* folder and on your **1st & 2nd Semester Incoming Monies Record** as the checks come in all summer.

Some scholarship awards come in as late as October or November of your freshman year in college. They may state that the money is for *after* December 15—or the second semester. Go through each letter and highlight any action that needs to be taken by you. For example, they may ask you to send your official first-semester college transcript along with an official enrollment verification or course schedule for your *second* semester in order to receive your check. Complete these tasks as early as possible and record the action taken.

This record is an important paper to be filled out and totaled each semester. You may find a year in college where the balances are out of whack! You see that most of your outside private scholarship money is coming in your second semester, and when you add up your college and federal money, you actually have more money than you need for your second semester bill and not enough for your first semester bill.

Because you are a *working partner* with your college, most of the time they are willing to shift what *they* are giving you in your second semester to your first semester, thus balancing everything out. They want you to continue applying for outside private scholarship money, because that way you help them accept and help another student.

● A PDF of the **1st & 2nd Semester Incoming Monies Record Sample** is available at www.JoanCRyan.com or on the CD-ROM at the back of this book.

Some Debt-Reducing Tips

L ife doesn't always go as smoothly as we'd like, and for college monies, some juggling may be needed to cover expenses. Here are some ideas for both parents and students to reduce the debt incurred in the pursuit of a college education.

For Parents

Write a letter to the financial aid director and follow up with a phone call. Politeness, kindness, and courtesy count—*a lot!* Don't even try to be aggressive or slick. Compose a letter requesting appeal of your financial aid award. Use key terminology such as, "My wife and I have *exhausted* all avenues for paying the balance... More special circumstances have occurred... increased health insurance costs..."

Ask if the college has any "Special Talent" money available? Are there any campus jobs that offer free or reduced tuition? (Parent, this means *you*. You could work on campus to help defray tuition costs. Tuition is often waived or reduced for students whose parents are employed at the school.) Is there an option of a cooperative program, larger federal student loan, federal work–study, or double major?

Would the school send you information on *unusual* scholarships? (Yes, there are scholarships for such categories as left-handed students, students with all Cs, and those who are over 6′2″ tall.) Is there a college scholarship booklet or website you could research

> *There are scholarships for... left-handed students, students with all Cs, and those who are over 6′2″ tall.*

for inside private scholarships? What does the school's business office offer for matching scholarships or internships, paid and unpaid? Can an appointment be arranged to look through the matching grant book in the business office?

Contact the department head of your student's major in person to ask about any kind of money that might be available, such as departmental scholarships, grants, internships, or sponsorships.

Research your state's educational financial web site to see if any opportunities exist there.

FOR STUDENTS

1. Take general core courses at a community college during the summer. Send community college course information to your primary college Admissions director in advance and for confirmation of transfer of credits for that course.
2. Use the College Level Examination Program (CLEP). Take exam, pass exam, *and* get college credits.
3. Take a double major.
4. Do not have a student car on campus.
5. Check out *College First* military money.
6. Obtain a certificate or license to qualify for specialized campus jobs, such as computer help, sign language, tutoring the disabled, lifeguarding at the pool.
7. Increase your GPA and class rank.
8. Complete your degree requirements in three years instead of four by taking 20 credits per year.
9. National Guard Reserves money.
10. Self-employment.
11. Paid internships.
12. Corporate sponsors.

MORE REVENUE-GENERATING IDEAS

Approach this endeavor—the scholarship process—as a lucrative part-time job in itself.

If you have been applying for outside private scholarships since high school, you know the drill. Keep in constant communication with your financial aid director for financial aid award updates and changes. You have experience. You can hire yourself! Look at how much money you earned by looking at your final annual financial aid award letter, your final 1st and 2nd Semester Incoming Monies Record, and your final college tuition graph sheets.

Set up three envelopes for yourself.

1. Into one envelope, deposit your summer work income for "spending allowance money at college." Budget it for nine months. For example, if you need $50 a week ($200 a month), you need to save around $1,800.

2. The second envelope is for private scholarship checks that are not needed for college tuition and can be used for unexpected or added expenses, such as study abroad.

3. A third envelope is for unexpected money—say, birthday, Christmas, or graduation money. This envelope should be labelled "Stafford Loan Repayment Money" and dated with the year of your graduation. This money could be put toward paying on your *final* Stafford debt balance. Plan not to touch this money for four years—just keep adding to it and keep it in a safe box.

Everyone in the family—mom, dad, and student—needs to have a large glass jar, and every time you empty your pocket, put the change into it. At the end of every summer, cash in the jars at the bank and put this money in your "Stafford Loan Repayment Money."

> *Everyone in the family—mom, dad, and student— needs to have a large glass jar.*

Open up a Christmas Club account at your bank, set a savings goal, and then pay into the account to try to reach the goal. Or you could take the money out in November and put it toward your second-semester tuition bill.

If you are not good at managing money or none of these suggestions interests you, make this your own challenge—like a game you are trying to win: use your own creativity in setting up a plan.

Instead of working at McDonald's full-time and attending college full-time, work at McDonald's part-time and apply for outside private scholarships part-time—in your dorm on your own time. Your self-employment partner is probably your mom, your teammate. There are skills and duties she can do from her at-home file box that align with what you are doing with your portable file box. Because your mother has identical contents, there will be times when she can take over. If you are ill or when exam time comes and you need to fully devote yourself to study, you can. She can take over from her base of operations.

You can divide job responsibilities: The student's job can be the **"document supplier."** At college, you are privy to the official transcript, official enrolled course schedule, letters of recommendation from professors, the official financial aid award letter, at-college extra-curricular activities verification, and photos of you taken at college. You make a copy of all of these documents for your portable file box and send the original and a copy of all of these documents to your mom on a regular basis each semester, and she can incorporate them into her at-home file box.

Mom's job is the **"package mailer and record keeper."** Law Number 1 applies here (copy everything!). When she receives your *original* documents, she needs to file those in the safe box and use the copy you sent as a working copy. She needs to weed out old documents and insert new, updated ones. You'll then have the same materials in your boxes. Deadline dates demand it.

Check out our PDF document titled, **A Student's Perspective, Laurie Coco.** It will give you insights about a student's experience—one who's lived it firsthand.

● A PDF of the **A Student's Perspective, Laurie Coco** is available at www.JoanCRyan.com or on the CD-ROM at the back of this book.

A Quick Refresher

Students, remember to apply for private scholarship money a year before you need it—*every year*. But for your first year at college, its imperative you stay ahead of the game. If you don't, you could find yourself without the financial resources to attend school. It takes *discipline* and *tenacity*—both traits that will keep you in good stead and translate into your being able to sleep at night, knowing you can focus on school rather than finances.

Your Schedule in a Nutshell

July, before your college freshman classes: Change your Personal Profile Paper by taking out the name and address of your high school and inserting your college. You can update your photo and FAQ form, too.

August: Prepare your shorter, customized scholarship list. You'll need envelopes, the Standard Request Letters, and self-addressed stamped envelopes to send out applications for your sophomore year. Have your mom mail these after Labor Day.

September: Go to college.

October: Study and supply your mom with college documents needed to apply for private scholarships.

November: Study, come home, and enjoy Thanksgiving.

December: Before you go home on Christmas break, write a *progress note* with some interesting, storytelling photos. When you arrive home, create "progress packets" for every scholarship family, foundation, or association from whom you received an award. Pull up the window shade of your first semester year at college to let these kind, generous people in. Let them see your fears, struggles, accomplishments, and growth. These scholarship committee volunteers will be keeping you in your college seat year after year. Remember, it is only common courtesy, when someone gives you their money, to send a handwritten thank-you note

> *Let them see your fears, struggles, accomplishments, and growth.*

and a progress note with photos each December and May. Hopefully, some day you, too, will become a scholarship committee volunteer who changes students' lives for the better.

Place at least three, official first-semester college transcripts into your at-home and portable scholarship boxes. Open one and make copies. Update your Personal Profile Paper, sports resume, art resume, and other papers with new information.

January: Parents need to meet with their accountant for current educational tax credits, deductions, or programs. Also, with your accountant, fill out FAFSA/SAR, the Unusual Circumstance paper, and any college financial aid office verification forms. Update your income tax forms, SAR, and CSS Financial Profile, and weed out old papers from both file boxes.

February and March: When you receive new financial aid award letters, do the same drill that you did when you were a high school senior. Fill out annual tuition graph papers. Sign and accept college monies.

April and May: Place at least three official first- and second-semester college transcripts into your at-home and portable scholarship folders. Open one and make copies. Weed out old transcripts. Make a doctor's appointment for a complete physical and update your vaccines. Work, intern, shadow, and volunteer.

June: Attend private scholarship award ceremonies and send thank-you notes. Update your Incoming and Outgoing budget numbers, your first- and second-semester incoming monies sheet, and your college tuition graph sheets for sophomore year.

July, having completed your freshman year: You and your parents work together on updating the frequently asked questions (FAQ), place the original in your vault, and both of you keep a duplex copy at hand in a plastic sheet cover.

August: Get ready for the new school year. Buy supplies, create new lists, and send out Standard Request Letters. Record and repeat these steps year after year, learning valuable skills that will serve you for the rest of your life.

IT'S A FAMILY AFFAIR—BONDING WITH YOUR TEEN

In our country, it has become commonplace for parents to have a difficult relationship with their teenage children. Working on the scholarship process, with the entire family directly involved in every part of the footwork—from middle school age onward—creates a tight family bond. That bond is a direct result of *teamwork*.

The family becomes one unit—parents, children, grandparents, great-grandparents—all working together toward a common goal. A client I once had was a parent who worked so many jobs and such long hours that he did not really know his daughter, a high school senior. From the time she was very young, until late in her high school career, he was unable to be involved in her life. But sometimes life circumstances change everything. As it turned out for this father and daughter, life threw them a curve ball that ended up as a home run.

Sherry, who was interested in attending a school in New York, was required to participate in an interview for a very substantial private scholarship. She needed her father to drive her there and back from New Hampshire, which he did. The day after they returned from this interview, the father phoned me to say he could care less if his daughter ever received the scholarship because something far more important had taken place—they had become re-acquainted.

If he and his daughter had not gone through this scholarship process, which precipitated the drive, he would have missed the opportunity to know his daughter well. During the car ride down and back to New York, he and his daughter had discussed their whole lives—things that were important to both of them—and they bonded in a way that neither of them expected. Two strangers became very good friends, all because of a private scholarship interview ride.

THE BOTTOM LINE

As the sage Ovid said many centuries ago, "Nothing worth having was ever achieved without effort." And so it is with the scholarship process.

The experience, strength, and hope provided in this book serves as a guide. It offers tried and true suggestions for you, the student, and you, the parents, to bring your own creativity, common sense, and imagination into the process of the three steps described here.

> *Nothing worth having was ever achieved without effort. —Ovid*

Trust people. Respect people. Honor people. Trust the process. Respect the process. Honor the process. Inside these three steps, there is a wide berth for you to customize your own path to your chosen opportunities.

The hardest challenge is to be yourself in a world where everyone is trying to make you somebody else.
                                        —e.e. cummings

The key to success is not to look outward at what colleges or financial aid directors might want. Look inward with rigorous honesty, and approach your goal to obtain a college or vocational education with confidence and conviction. Treat your core values as sacred. You will find your own power *inside* you.

Present the best about yourself in a way that pleases you. Give to others what you would want them to give you. Even with all our advanced technology, this educational process is still a human being to human being experience.

And that is a good thing.

APPENDIX

USING YOUR DATA TO APPLY FOR A JOB

During the recession that started in 2008, some of my clients found themselves without work and unable to find a job. It was even harder for students. We found that much of the process in this book could be applied to the job search, particularly in preparing your materials for your prospective employer. We had considerable success. This appendix leads you through the documents you'll need to land that job.

THE COVER LETTER

The **cover letter** accompanying your resume is the first piece of the package and should draw your reader in. Get right to the point. Keep it to just one page—less is more.

First paragraph. Start with, "I am interested in your job position because..." Tell the reader a story. Then WWWWH (who, what, why, when, and how).

Second paragraph. "I qualify because..."

Third paragraph. "I have enclosed as much information about myself as possible so that you may come to a confident decision with regard to hiring me. If, however, you have any questions at all, I would be happy to answer them for you. My phone number is... My email address is... Thank you for considering me as a candidate for your (name the job title you're applying for)."

THE PERSONAL PROFILE PAPER

The Personal Profile Paper needs to be informative, interesting, varied, and non-repetitive. By sharing all of you with your prospective employer, you will be setting yourself apart from the long line of candidates applying for the same job. Do not bold your name—bold only the categories you have chosen for your paper. Keep it short—just one page. Imagine that your reader may be someone higher up in the company whom you will not ever meet in person. This Personal Profile is an interview on paper—it is not a resume and should not resemble a resume. The casual photo can be included.

> *This Personal Profile is an interview on paper—it is not a resume.*

In a job interview, it is commonplace to be asked, "What do you do outside of work?" The Personal Profile Paper is a good place to answer this question. Take time here to describe your family—they will be on this employment journey right alongside you. Answer other questions, such as "What interests do you have?" "Do you have any hobbies?" (Perhaps the company hosts an employee hobby day.) Have you pursued different educational interests?" (Perhaps they could use your accounting skills for their employee volunteer program.) "Do you serve on a committee in your parish?" "Are you an efficiency expert of sorts?" "Are you involved in sports? (Their company has an employee baseball game every summer.) "Have you travelled? What did you learn from your travel experiences?" (Perhaps the company could use employees that speak other languages.) "Are you musical? (Their employees play their musical instruments during their employee annual Christmas Party.)

ESSAYS

Show your employer who you are with the following five written pieces.

1. Write a **"core" paper** of persuasion, passion, and conviction about you. Keep it to one page and include where you were, where you are, and where you hope to be. It should be a paper of the past, present, and future.

    Not all of us have a pristine past. Some may have a past criminal record. If so, address that issue right up front in the essay. Be brief. Be clear. Be honest. No excuses. Then move on to where you are now. Again, three paragraphs only. Writing on one page, communicating in three paragraphs, shows your prospective employer that you can deliver information honestly and concisely. This would add to your employment position.

2. A **"slice of life" paper**. One small event in your life that was important to you.

3. **"Obstacles I've overcome" paper**. Keep the key emphasis on "overcome."

4. The **"graded essay"** needs to be a copy of an interesting essay graded by your teacher, professor, or instructor.

5. Your **"employment resume"** needs to be one page only—unless you are 92 years old, then two pages.

BIBLIOGRAPHY

- If you're an artist, list the names of your pieces. Enclose images of these works on a CD-ROM.

- List the titles of the songs you perform in your repertoire and enclose pictures of your recitals.

- List the names, dates, places, and awards you have won for, say, race car driving. Enclose pictures of you holding your trophy.

SPECIAL SKILL CERTIFICATES

If you have special skills, mention them. Here are some examples:

Because of my Mohawk heritage, I have no problem with height and tall buildings. My insides were built for height. I am always chosen to work at the top of skyscrapers.

I am proficient in the Navajo Code language and am able to work with language translators.

List what degree of proficiency you have in scuba diving, copy the certificate, and show a photo of places and events in which you have participated.

SUMMARY OF QUALIFICATIONS PAPER

- Leadership skills in the job position you are now seeking
- Experience in that environment
- Field performances
- Professional development through continued education
- News articles and photos, including the name of the newspaper or magazine and date, connected to your leadership, experience, field performance, and professional development.

OTHER INFORMATION

Annual Salary Information: If you know the salary information on the prospective position, it may indicate a range. Depending upon your length of experience and depth of knowledge, you may want to show why you would be interested in the higher range.

Benefits Information Package: One of the first questions you may be asked in an interview is what interests you have outside of work. If the answer is family, then you need to read up on what family benefits the prospective employer offers. Have it in writing: it is one thing to be offered information verbally and quite another to have it in black and white.

Credit Report—FICO scores: Request your free credit reports from Experian, TransUnion, and Equifax. And you will have all three credit report agencies' report to check and correct if you find errors.

It is important for a person who is applying for a new job to be in the best possible position mentally, physically, spiritually, emotionally, and financially. This brings with it tremendous confidence and positivity, which is always an asset.

According to the Equal Employment Opportunity Commission (EEOC), 87 percent of employers use the credit report *after* conditional offers of employment or interviews. This report will list all former employers and display how you handle money.

Letters of Recommendation: Create an introduction package about yourself to send to someone who might recommend you. It should include your Personal Profile Paper, essay, news articles, copies of awards, certificates, and diplomas. Let your recommender know a lot about you so she can comment on all those areas in her letter of recommendation.

Personnel Annual Evaluation Reports: Save your copies.

Personal Statement: People change. We go through life learning from our mistakes. If you have a past employment record that you are not proud of, write a paper about it right up front. What have you learned from your experiences, and what kind of employee are you now?

Position Applied For: Be clear about the job description and qualifications. Apply as early as possible. Be ready.

Required Signatures, Notary Public, Special Documents: Check instructions for job application requirements.

Union Membership: Consult with a union steward.

ON UNEMPLOYMENT BENEFITS?

Don't just sit at the computer sending out a gazillion resumes. Think about a place where you would love to work. Get all dressed up, briefcase filled with your employment package, and apply for a volunteer position at that company. Firm handshake, eye contact, and bounding enthusiasm count.

Then, while some unemployed people head for the couch and the antidepressants, you will be receiving a paycheck (your unemployment check) while enjoying working at a place you love. After volunteering for awhile, you can inquire about internships—either paid and unpaid. You can determine if this company and environment are truly where your soul is satisfied and where you effortlessly make important contributions.

All people have unique gifts and talents, so try to get a potential employer to see that.

Look at who and what you are. If you have a hobby that you pursue, maybe you really love it. Why not clear out your garage and set up a business all about your hobby and hang out your shingle?

● PDFs of **Employment Document Sample List** and **Employment Document Checklist** are available at www.JoanCRyan.com or on the CD-ROM at the back of this book.

INDEX OF PDFS

The page numbers in this index indicate the book page references for the PDFs on the CD-ROM or web site.

ABOUT THE AUTHOR

For Joan Catherine Ryan, *Scholarship Matters: A Parent's Guide to College and Private Scholarships* is the realization of a dream and the culmination of research that spans over twenty years. It is telling that she lists her most important positions as daughter, mother, mother-in-law, and grandmother. *Scholarship Matters* is, indeed, a labor of love.

The author was inspired by her own life experiences. Unlike some other how-to books, this one is completely "road-tested." It includes the steps that Joan, herself, found to be most successful. She went back to school herself at 47, attending Northern Essex Community College in Haverhill, Massachusetts from 1989 to 1994. Before she sat in her first college class, she had secured five private scholarships for herself. Joan then studied Advanced Grant Writing at the University of New Hampshire in 1994. In 1995, she completed the Papoutsy Business Seminar for Women Entrepreneurs.

As a single mother, she knew that finding and securing college scholarship funding for her children was tantamount. Working as a team with her daughter Catherine, Joan turned her expertise into a foolproof system for applying and securing scholarship money to defray the high cost of Catherine's education.

Over the years, Joan met other parents facing the daunting task of funding their children's education. She decided to use her experience to help them. In 2004, she started her own consulting business, The Scholarship Counselor, Preparer for College Admissions and Private Scholarships, in Hampton,

New Hampshire. Since then, she has served as a successful mentor, helping other parents to achieve what she did for her own family.

This book is the natural progression for Joan Ryan. Drawing on her own experiences as well as those of other parents, Joan has created a practical tool for parents feeling "at sea" with the overwhelming process of college admissions. *Scholarship Matters* demystifies the process and makes the journey so much easier.

Joan C. Ryan has received the following awards: Thanks Be to Grandmother Winifred Foundation Award, Jeanette Rankin National Scholarship Mary Myers Award, Northern Essex Community College Alumni Award, Fitch Memorial Scholarship Award, and the Scholarship Foundation of America Semi-Finalist.

She was also chosen as one of the "Women of the 21st Century," by the Harvard-Radcliffe–Schlesinger Library Committee.

Photo © Phillip Noury, Austin Studios

About the Author's Daughter

Catherine Meinen credits her mother with her joy of learning and love of motherhood.

While attending high school, Catherine and her mother worked together to select, apply to, and secure the funds necessary to attend college. Catherine was welcomed into Gordon College and earned her BA in Biblical and Theological Studies, with a Judaic Studies concentration. She went on to earn her MA in Education and enjoyed teaching middle school students for several years.

She now is fully engaged in raising her toddler son, Camden, and her four-year-old daughter, Zoe, who is recovering from brain cancer. Her experience with the steps in this book have helped her navigate the medical and social service agency realms necessary to care for her daughter.

NOTES

NOTES

NOTES

NOTES

NOTES

NOTES